T0017614

Jonathan Edwards was a burning and shining light of spiritual truth. However, it can be daunting to read a sermon by an eighteenth-century theologian. Imagine, though, sitting with a friend, reading a page or two of Edwards, and talking together about what it means and how it applies. That is the sweet experience of reading this book, with Deborah Howard as our personal guide to one of the greatest preachers of all time. The questions for reflection at the end of each section make this a helpful study for small groups as well.

Dr. Joel R. Beeke
President, Puritan Reformed Theological Seminary,
Grand Rapids, Michigan

Deborah Howard's book, *Jonathan Edwards and The Christian Pilgrim*, brings to life, through practical application and her personal experiences, Jonathan Edwards' sermon by the same name. For example, Edwards states:

> When we are called to any secular business, or charged with the care of a family [and] if we improve our lives to any other purpose than as a journey toward heaven, all our labor will be lost.

Howard's comment on that sentence:

> That's why we're not to focus so much on this world we live in, on the possessions He's given us, or on the families and friends we're a part of. Edwards repeatedly advises us to be ready to leave everything behind when our time comes to depart—and to do it joyfully. . . Only one answer suffices. We are to be busy about the works of righteousness He has already planned for us—and those works are different for each of us. Our lives are to be a witness for and to Him.

Howard uses her personal experience as a hospice nurse to her advantage as she brings Edwards' treasures alive for our day. She uses the Scripture well and adds helpful discussion questions at the end of each chapter.

I enjoyed the way Howard comments on Edwards' conclusion by likening death to the birth of a baby. That baby feels comfortable in his or her environment but of necessity must move on to its next stage of life. "Like that little baby, there comes a time when we have no choice but to step through the corridor—and also like that baby we will find a place superior to anything we've known before, a place where we feel more at home than ever, feel more love and joy than ever, and are brought face-to-face with the One who loved us before the creation of the world and breathed life into us—both physically and spiritually. What an astonishing thought."

I highly recommend her book.

Michael Brunk
Pastor, Kathorus Bible Church, Johannesburg, South Africa

If the last few years have taught us anything, it's that life is frail and temporary and that death is coming for every single one of us. Only through the finished and sufficient work of Christ can the Christian look death in the face with hope in the face of loss and grief and know with confidence they will be with Christ forever. In her latest book, *Jonathan Edwards and The Christian Pilgrim,* Deborah Howard helps the reader through a combination of using a sermon by the greatest pastor-theologian America has ever produced, Jonathan Edwards, and her commentary on that sermon to navigate the challenges of grief and loss associated with death with hope in Christ. Along the way in Deborah's book, you'll discover not only the hope that Christ provides for the future but the hope that He offers now. The hope that we have now is because of Christ, and the hope we have for the future is because of Christ. Everywhere in between now and the future, Christ offers hope for those whose friends and family have passed on. Deborah has done us a great service with this book for the hurting, the struggler, and the biblical counselor. Please read this book and know that the hope you have now in Christ is the hope that Christ holds you fast now, and He will continue to hold you fast till your last breath. Then you will breathe your last and go into His everlasting arms if you are in Christ forever. Reading this book will help you enter into the world of Edwards, and into the eternal life revealed in Scripture for both now and forever, because Christ alone is sufficient for now and forever.

Dave Jenkins
Executive Director, Servants of Grace Ministries,
Author, *The Word Explored* and *The Word Matters*

Deborah Howard has done it again. She's written another compassionate work that points us to our Savior, Jesus Christ. My wife and I think it's fantastic. God has given her a gift which she uses to encourage, inform and inspire. What she has done with this Jonathan Edwards' sermon is very fine, indeed. We heartily recommend this book to all believers.

Dr. Wayne Mack
Association of Certified Biblical Counselors (ACBC) Academy member,
Director, ACBC Africa;
elder and pastor, Lynnwood Baptist Church, Pretoria, South Africa

Deborah Howard has produced another wonderful, encouraging and convicting work. As her father, a committed believer, was dying recently, her attention was drawn to Jonathan Edwards' message, "The Christian Pilgrim." Deborah intersperses her own comments into Edwards' sermon, clarifying and adding current relevance to his words. Drawing from her experience as a hospice nurse, attending to many who were in the process of dying, she causes us to think about our own eventual deaths, about preparing for death as a believer, and laying out before us the joys of what it will be like when we meet the Lord for an eternity. Deborah, in her kind way, is very convicting as she writes of the responsibilities and joys of keeping eternity and heaven ever before us. And at the end, she issues a warning to those who live only for themselves and who are not prepared to meet the Lord. Get a copy of this book, read it, then pass it along to someone who may need this message.

Curtis Thomas

Retired pastor and co-author of *Romans: An Interpretive Outline and The Five Points of Calvinism: Defined, Defended and Documented*

Our Journey Towards Heaven

Jonathan Edwards

and the

Christian Pilgrim

Deborah Howard

CHRISTIAN
FOCUS

Copyright © Deborah Howard 2023

hardback ISBN 978-1-5271-0978-0
ebook ISBN 978-1-5271-1033-5

Published in 2023 by
Christian Focus Publications Ltd,
Geanies House, Fearn, Ross-shire,
IV20 1TW, Great Britain.
www.christianfocus.com

Cover design by James Amour

Printed and bound by Gutenberg Press Ltd, Malta

Contents

Dedicated to my father,
Joe G. Koon
1931 – 2020

FOREWORD

Death. It is rightly called "the king of terrors." The Bible calls it, "The last enemy." Unless the Lord returns soon, we must all finally face this terrifying enemy. Part of the challenge in this final encounter lies in the fact that it is a painful experience as the spirit escapes the body that has been its house from the beginning. Therefore, in 2 Corinthians 5, the apostle Paul spoke in terms of us not wishing to be unclothed but to be clothed with our heavenly dwelling. The unclothing is not desired by anyone. Yet, we cannot get into our heavenly clothing without first being unclothed. It is this phenomenon of the unclothing of the soul that this book addresses.

As a pastor, I have been by the bedside of children of God as they have been in the throes of death. Often, they are surrounded by a few people who have done all they could to prevent them from coming to this point of departure. They have poured in their loving care and their finances to bring in the best doctors. But when the day assigned by the Lord for our departure from this world arrives, there is nothing anyone can do to prevent death—that awful reaper—from doing what it knows best. I have watched helplessly as the person whose love and fellowship we had learned to treasure passed from this life into the next. How can anyone ever get used to or be ready for such a moment?

Whereas we can never get used to death, we can be made ready for it through meditating deeply on the Christian's blessed hope. This may be done through drawing from the rich reservoir of Christian hymnody. Many psalms, hymns and spiritual songs were written by Christians who looked death in the face and defied its terror through the cross. As Spafford triumphantly writes, "The sky, not the grave, is our goal." When we sing such songs by the bedside of a departing saint, they can be a great source of consolation for both the departing saint and for those who are remaining behind.

Yet another source of this assurance of better things awaiting the saints after the final battle with death are sermons that are rich with the unsearchable treasures of Christ. Today, the availability of the internet enables anyone anywhere—including on a deathbed in a hospital or hospice—to listen to the most soul-assuring messages available in the world. While the body is growing weaker and weaker, and the end not far out of sight, headphones can pipe into the soul messages about the glory that awaits the saint and cause the child of God to long for heaven.

I would, however, not want to limit listening to such messages to the time when one is on the eve of their departure from this life. This is because part of the consolation from such hymns and sermons comes from a life that was not wasted chasing after the froth and dew of this world. The consolation partly comes from a life spent in faithful service for God and for the extension of His kingdom in the various fields He has placed us. That is partly what makes a child of God look forward to hearing those words, "Well done, good and faithful servant!"

Thus, I would encourage believers to meditate on the life to come even when their health is robust so that they can spend and be spent about the Master's business. That way, when health begins to fail, and they listen to messages about heaven, they will not bemoan a wasted life. Rather, they will be glad to know they are now about to enter into their eternal reward.

That is how it was with the apostle Paul. Part of his final consolation lay in giving us a peek into a life that was well-lived. He wrote, "I have fought the good fight, I have finished the race, I have kept the faith. Henceforth there is laid up for me the crown of righteousness, which the Lord, the righteous judge, will award to me on that day, and not only to me but also to all who have loved his appearing," (2 Tim. 4:7-8). May we live well so that we may also die well!

What Deborah Howard does in this book is to go back to those days when audio and video technology did not exist and pick a sermon by the great Jonathan Edwards for the purpose of encouraging dying saints. Edwards is best known for his sermon, "Sinners in the hands of an angry God." Yet, he was not just a hellfire and brimstone preacher. He was also a compassionate pastor. He drew from Scripture truths that nourished the souls of believers, including those who were staring death in the face. The sermon picked by Deborah Howard is in that category.

By adding her own comments to the sermon, she not only enables us to understand some of the quaint sayings but also personalizes the truths in the sermon so that we can feel something of their present-day application. As a hospice nurse of many years, having seen hundreds of people breathe their last, she does so with an authenticity that will touch the heart of any reader.

This is the kind of book that you would want to put by the bedside of a terminally ill child of God so that those who are providing tender loving care can read short sections to encourage the one who is currently in the valley of the shadow of death. For all human beings, death is not the end. It is the start of a new phase of life that was being prepared for here on earth. For those who die outside Christ, it is the start of everlasting punishment. But for the Christian, it is the start of everlasting and unalloyed joy.

It is the latter that is explored by the sermon in this book written by one of the greatest minds that ever graced this planet, Jonathan Edwards. Read it now for yourself even if you are in the best of health. Keep it in your treasure chest for that day when you will need to encourage God's children on the brink of eternity. Yes, keep it there for the day when you will need someone else to read it to you afresh when your day comes to say farewell to this world.

Dr. Conrad Mbewe
Pastor at Kabwata Baptist Church and Founding
Chancellor of the African Christian University in Lusaka,
Zambia

INTRODUCTION

We are dying. All of us.

Death is inevitable. People differ in their preparedness for it. Some give it no thought at all. Others obsess over it. Still others live by the motto, "Eat, drink and be merry for tomorrow we die." They want to grab all the gusto they can get out of this life because, to them, this is all there is.

People may "put their ducks in a row." They may "put their affairs in order." They may write wills, leave trusts, and prearrange their funeral and burial. Then they can place a big checkmark that states, "Done." But is that all there is? Are these final measures the most we can do to prepare for such a momentous occurrence? How does "the end" affect their living?

What about spiritual preparedness? Is there a balanced way to look at death—a way that prepares us and honors God? A marquee in front of a local church said, "Live with the end in sight." I thought, "Wow, what a gruesome idea." However, the more I thought about it, the better I liked it.

You see, it depends on how you define "the end." Is death the end? Or is it life *after* death? We are all dying. Then again, we're all eternal beings. Where we spend eternity depends on what we've done with our lives on earth. Ultimately, it depends on whether we obeyed God's call to believe in Him, to trust Him as our Savior.

Though none of us have the ability in and of ourselves to obey Him, He provides the ability by choosing His elect from among mankind, by sending His Son to redeem His people, and by sending the Holy Spirit to efficaciously draw those He loves to Him. Only then are we given eyes that can see His truth and hearts that can turn to Him in faith and repentance, believing in Him as our Lord and Savior.

If we're believers in Jesus Christ we have no end. Death is but a doorway for us that leads to heaven and our Lord. We step through it to eternal bliss. Death is also a doorway for unbelievers—but once they step through it, they step into the abyss of eternal damnation.

Some people turn thoughts of death into a morbid fixation—death, death, death and then the grave, followed by black nothingness. Black hair, black eyeliner, black nail polish, black clothes, dark circles under the eyes, black hat. Gloom and doom. But is that how believers are to approach death? No. Believers understand that death is not the end.

Living with the end in sight doesn't mean thinking of death all the time. It means thinking of what comes *after* death—eternal life in heaven with our Savior, Jesus Christ. We are to strive to do what Colossians 3:1-2 says, "If then you have been raised with Christ, seek the things that are above, where Christ is, seated at the right hand of God. Set your minds on things that are above, not on things that are on earth."

Before we can truly set our minds on things above and not upon things of this life, we must heed the first part of the verse. We must be raised to life with Him. Therefore, I'm writing primarily to Christians, to God's elect. Only they will have the capability to view life and death through the spiritual lens Jonathan Edwards saw through when he wrote this sermon. Yet, unbelievers may also profit from this outstanding sermon, especially if it causes them to think about what lies ahead.

As a hospice nurse for over twenty-five years, I've had far more exposure to death and dying than the average person. I've sat by hundreds of bedsides, held the hands of hundreds of people as they exited this world to step into the next. I suppose thoughts about death are an occupational hazard for hospice nurses.

I had the recent honor of sitting beside my father as he lay dying. Holding his hand, singing hymns, praying for him, and watching his spirit tear loose from his mortal flesh have made me suddenly more philosophical about the meaning of life and death.

Not that I'm not always philosophically and spiritually-minded when I think of such things. I've written about them. *Sunsets: Reflections for Life's Final Journey,* continues to be my most successful book.[1] It serves as a devotional as well as a nursing guidebook for walking that journey with a dying loved one. Yet, it is directed more toward the process of dying than it is about the life to follow.

---

1.   (Wheaton: Crossway, 2005)

My father's death brought this excellent sermon by Jonathan Edwards to mind. Once again, I was blessed by reading it. *To me it serves as a pep talk for heaven.*

As part of my daily devotions this year, I'm reading Paul David Tripp's *New Morning Mercies: A Daily Gospel Devotional.* His entry for September 18 echoes the principles of this book. He said, "Today remember that this moment isn't intended to be a destination, but it is what God's using to prepare you for your final destination." He goes on to explain what happens when we view this life as our destination.

Basically, he says if you live with a destination mentality:

- You are going to be regularly disappointed.
- You will have unrealistic expectations and you will not guard yourself against temptation as you should.
- You will struggle to believe that God is loving, good, faithful and kind.
- It will be easier for you to complain than to be content.
- You will be tempted to envy the life of someone else.
- You will tend to hook your happiness to the degree of ease and comfort that you experience in your present situations and relationships.
- You simply won't be on God's agenda page at all.

He writes,

> Living with a destination mentality means that you load all your hopes and dreams, your search for a definition of the good life, and your inner sense of well-being into this present moment. It means that no matter what your

theology says about eternity, you live as if this is all there is. And because you are living as if this is all there is, you try to turn this present moment in this fallen world into the paradise that it will never be. Yes, if you are God's child, you have been promised a paradise beyond your ability to conceive, but you must understand that this is not it. This sin-broken world, populated by sin-scarred people, will never be the paradise that you and I tend to long for it to be. You see, a sound biblical doctrine of the future is the only way to arrive at a sound biblical understanding of the present. . .. So don't try to turn today into paradise, but thank God that you are being prepared by grace for the paradise that will be your forever home."[2]

Edwards would have heartily approved of this passage in Tripp's book. He believed that, too. The things of this world are nothing compared to the bliss of our eternity with Christ.

Edwards lived with the end in sight—not a morbid fascination with death, but an excitement and enthusiasm about the eternity beyond. His joyful exuberance for heaven, more than anything else, dictated the joyful way he lived his life. That life, lived 300 years ago, serves as a terrific encouragement and example for believers. It is as relevant and inspiring today as it was then. In writing this book I hope to introduce this marvelous sermon to others, and to deliver an encouraging word to this generation of dying people.

Jonathan Edwards fixed his eyes upon God. Like John Bunyan, writer of *Pilgrim's Progress,* Edwards viewed the Christian life as a journey to a final destination. Certainly, *Pilgrim's Progress* must have influenced his

---

2.   Tripp, Paul David, *New Morning Mercies: A Daily Gospel Devotional.* (Wheaton, IL: Crossway, 2014). September 18 entry.

thoughts and ideas. In that book, Christian's journey toward the Celestial City is like our own pilgrimage to our heavenly abode, encountering dangers and blessing along the way.

We are also guided by the Spirit, held secure by God's righteous right hand and delivered safely to our final destination. Edwards understood this better than most, and, oh, the joy he experienced when considering this heavenly home! You'll see that clearly in this sermon.

Can we attain to Jonathan Edwards' glorious, entranced view of the glory of heaven? Can we love God as he loved God? Can our joy derive from God's very existence, from His holiness, from His excellencies? Can we do it perfectly?

Probably not. However, Edwards' writings give us a high standard to strive for. The blessing is in the striving. He shows us what it means to truly live our lives with the end in sight. And what is the end? Death? No, GLORY. Those who belong to the King of Heaven will dwell in His glory for all eternity.

This was the source of Jonathan Edwards' joy. This foundation cannot be shaken, a truth that never fades, and cannot be destroyed. When your heart is fixed upon this truth, nothing that happens in this life will be able to separate you from that exquisite joy.

So now let me introduce you to this wonderful sermon. (To prevent any confusion, the sermon by Edwards has been placed in a different font from my commentary on it.)

CHAPTER ONE

INTRODUCTION AND SECTION I

Hebrews 11:13-14[1]

And confessed that they were strangers and pilgrims on the earth. For they that say such things, declare plainly that they seek a country.

Subject: This life might so to be spent by us as to be only a journey towards heaven.

The apostle is here setting forth the excellencies of the grace of faith, by the glorious effects and happy issue of it in the saints of the Old Testament. He had spoken in the preceding part of the chapter particularly, of Abel, Enoch, Noah, Abraham, and Sarah, Isaac, and Jacob. Having enumerated those instances, he takes notice that "these all died in faith, not having received the promises, but having seen them afar off, were persuaded of them, and embraced them, and confessed that they were strangers," etc.—In these words the apostle seems to have a more particular respect to Abraham and Sarah, and their kindred, who came with them from Haran, and from Ur of the Chaldees, as appears by the 15th verse, where the

---

1. "All Scripture quotations within Jonathan Edwards sermon are from the King James Version."

apostle says, "and truly if they had been mindful of that country from whence they came out, they might have had opportunity to have returned."

Edwards begins his sermon by reminding us of the great Hall of Faith in Hebrews 11. He makes the point that all these people lived with their eyes fixed on a hope they never saw come to pass in their own lives. Yet they looked forward to that promise in faith.

That's what we're to do. Yes, many of the promises these Old Testament saints were looking forward to have now come to pass—but not all.

We have the privilege of being able to look back in history to the birth, life, death and resurrection of our Lord Jesus. But we now join these in the Hall of Faith as we also look forward to other promises—the promise of the rapture, of the second coming of Christ, and of His eventual defeat of Satan. We look forward to a new heaven and a new earth.

Closer to home, perhaps, we look forward to being with Christ in spirit the moment we leave these earthly bodies in death. We haven't experienced it. So why do we believe it?

We believe because that's what we are told in God's Word—the Word He breathed into existence through the men He chose to write it. We believe because He says that's the way it will be. We believe because we love our Lord and trust in His promises. And we believe that with our whole hearts.

"For the Lord himself will descend from heaven with a cry of command, with the voice of an archangel, and with the sound of the trumpet of God. And the dead in Christ will rise first. Then we who are alive, who are left, will be caught up together with them in the clouds to meet the Lord in the air, and so we will always be with the Lord. Therefore encourage one another with these words," 1 Thess. 4:16-18.

That's what Jonathan Edwards does with this sermon—he encourages us with the promises of God regarding heaven.

The second point he brings up is that God brought them out from their own country and created from Abraham a new nation. Yet they lived physically as strangers in a new land. Spiritually, it is the same with us.

Our earthly existence is transitory. This world is not our "home." We are as strangers passing through. We belong elsewhere—and that truest home is in heaven with Christ.

Two things may be observed here:

1. What these saints confessed of themselves, *viz. that they were strangers and pilgrims on the earth.*—Thus we have a particular account concerning Abraham, "I am a stranger and a sojourner with you." (Gen. 23:4) And it seems to have been the general sense of the patriarchs, by what Jacob says to Pharaoh. "And Jacob said to Pharaoh, The days of the years of my pilgrimage are an hundred and thirty years; few and evil have the days of years of my life been, and have not attained to the days of the years of the life of my fathers in the days of their pilgrimage." (Gen. 47:9) "I am a stranger and a sojourner with thee, as all my fathers were." (Psa. 39:12)

2. The inference that the apostle draws from hence, *viz. that they sought another country as their home.* "For they that say such things, declare plainly that they seek a country." In confessing that they were strangers, they plainly declared that this is not their country, that this is not the place where they are at home. And in confessing themselves to be pilgrims, they declared plainly that this is not their settled abode, but that they have respect to some other country, which they seek, and to which they are traveling.

Perhaps we've become a bit too comfortable here in this life. We settle into homes, families, jobs, and interests and snuggle down into comfortable lives. We tend to become more egocentric than theocentric.

Jonathan Edwards (1703-1758) did not do this. He realized that this world is not our home. Salvation changes that. From the moment Christ becomes the Lord of our life, we are to be "set apart."

Abraham left his home and was drawn by God to a new land. He and his descendants were set apart by a number of factors—geography, culture, and most of all, a relationship with the true and living God. Almighty God made from one man an entire nation of people—the Jews.

In a similar way, Christians are also set apart. We are to live lives that are different from the world around us. We may have belonged to that world before, but once we're saved, we are no longer comfortable there. Now we belong to a different country, a different world. Our lives are changed eternally. These lives are to be characterized by love. We are set apart for Christ.

Again, the main difference between us and the world around us is the relationship we have with the true and living God.

As King David wrote, we are strangers and sojourners with God in the days of our own pilgrimage, (Ps. 39:12). A continuing theme throughout this sermon is that allusion to our lives as a pilgrimage towards the final destination.

We don't ultimately belong to this world. It is not our home. Our destination is heaven, and our citizenship is held securely there. In a sense, we are merely "passing through" this world, anxiously looking ahead towards our true country.

SECTION I

That this life ought to be so spent by us, as to be only a journey or pilgrimage towards heaven.

Here I would observe,

1. That we ought not to rest in the world and its enjoyments, but should desire heaven. We should "seek first the kingdom of God." (Mat. 6:33) We ought above all things to desire a heavenly happiness; to be with God and dwell with Jesus Christ. Though surrounded with outward enjoyments, and settled in families with desirable friends and relations, though we have companions whose society is delightful, and children in whom we see many promising qualifications, though we live by good neighbors, and are generally beloved where known, we ought not to take our rest in these things as our portion. We should be so far

25

> from resting in them, that we should desire to
> leave them all, in God's due time. We ought to
> possess, enjoy and use them, with no other view
> but readily to quit them, whenever we are called
> to it, and to change them willingly and cheerfully
> for heaven.

This is one of those passages that reflects the fact that my spiritual maturity is far short of Jonathan Edwards'. Yes, I can readily agree with "seek first the kingdom of God." And yes, I can see that we should value our presence in heaven more than any earthly enticements.

However, my close relationships are so precious to me that I could not honestly say that I desire to leave them. I'm willing to leave them. But do I truly desire it?

With my hospice background, I've been intimately involved with so many patients who have died that I've seen something common to each case. It doesn't matter how popular, how brilliant, how skilled, how funny, how rich, how good-looking, or how cultured a person has been in life. As they move toward death, things begin to drop away from them.

First, it's participation in the interests they've enjoyed over the years. Next comes loss of function and ability. They require more and more help from others to maintain a semblance of normalcy.

As their sickness progresses, people begin to drop away from their circle of acquaintances. In an ever-tightening circle, they have energy enough for only a few of the closest family or dearest friends. But finally, they only have the energy it takes to keep breathing.

At that moment a believer has only one possession they may cling to—their relationship with the Lord.

And in the end, their spirit gladly tears loose from their diseased dwelling and enters eternity through the doorway of death. In the end we find that all we have is Christ—and that He is enough.

Though I know the moment of my death will release me to heaven, where I long to be face-to-face with my Lord, I still cannot say my heart yearns to leave those I love behind. However, I suspect that when that moment comes, God will change my desires in an instant—and then I will eagerly long for it—as Jonathan Edwards did.

> For we know that if the tent that is our earthly home is destroyed, we have a building from God, a house not made with hands, eternal in the heavens. For in this tent we groan, longing to put on our heavenly dwelling, if indeed by putting it on we may not be found naked. For while we are still in this tent, we groan, being burdened—not that we would be unclothed, but that we would be further clothed, so that what is mortal may be swallowed up by life. He who has prepared us for this very thing is God, who has given us the Spirit as a guarantee. So we are always of good courage. We know that while we are at home in the body we are away from the Lord, for we walk by faith, not by sight. Yes, we are of good courage, and we would rather be away from the body and at home with the Lord. So whether we are at home or away, we make it our aim to please him.

This matches completely with what Jonathan Edwards believed and wrote about in this sermon. We are to long to be with the Lord. We are to be of good courage. We are to live lives that please our Master.

> A traveler is not wont to rest in what he meets with, however comfortable and pleasing, on the road. If he

passes through pleasant places, flowery meadows or shady groves, he does not take up his content in these things, but only takes a transient view of them as he goes along. He is not enticed by fine appearances to put off the thought of proceeding. No, but his journey's end is in his mind. If he meets with comfortable accommodations at an inn, he entertains no thought of settling there. He considers that these things are not his own, that he is but a stranger, and when he has refreshed himself, or tarried for a night, he is for going forward. And it is pleasant to him to think that so much of the way is gone.

So should we desire heaven more than the comforts and enjoyments of this life. The apostle mentions it as an encouraging, comfortable consideration to Christians, that they draw nearer their happiness. "Now is our salvation nearer than when we believed."—Our hearts ought to be loose to these things, as that of a man on a journey, that we may as cheerfully part with them whenever God calls. "But this I say, brethren, the time is short, it remaineth, that both they that have wives be as though they had none, and they that weep, as though they wept not; and they that rejoice, as though they rejoiced not; and they that buy, as though they possessed not; and they that use this world, as not abusing it; for the fashion of this world passeth away." (I Cor. 7:29-31) These things are only lent to us for a little while, to serve a present turn, but we should set our *hearts* on heaven, as our inheritance forever.

I love traveling. I think of myself as having an artistic temperament. I want to drink in the new experiences traveling affords me. Many of those "experiences" are in the area of dining. No chain restaurants for me. I look for "local flavor" as much as "local color."

I greedily absorb the sights and sounds, tastes, smells and colors along the way—the hotels, architecture, climate, geography, food and music. I like to imagine what it's like to live in whatever place I visit. Yet, like Edwards describes, my heart yearns for the final destination.

This is also our Christian pilgrimage. We can live and grow and accomplish great things in this life. We can enjoy the amenities God gives us along the way. But that final destination is where we want to be. That's where we set our hearts upon. And as he says repeatedly through this sermon, our "home" is not our current address. Our true home, our true destination, is heaven.

2. We ought to seek heaven, by traveling in the way that leads thither. This is a way of holiness. We should choose and desire to travel thither in this way and in no other, and part with all those carnal appetites which, as weights, will tend to hinder us. "Let us lay aside every weight, and the sin which doth so easily beset us, and let us run with patience the race set before us." (Heb 12:1) However pleasant the gratification of any appetite may be, we must lay it aside if it be a hindrance, or a stumbling block, in the way to heaven.

We should travel on in the way of obedience to all God's commands, even the difficult as well as the easy, denying all our sinful inclinations and interests. The way to heaven is ascending. We must be content to travel up hill, though it be hard and tiresome, and contrary to the natural bias of our flesh. We should follow Christ: the path he traveled, was the right way to heaven. We should take up our cross and follow him, in

> meekness and lowliness of heart, obedience and charity, diligence to do good, and patience under afflictions. The way to heaven is a heavenly life, an imitation of those who are in heaven in their holy enjoyments, loving, adoring, serving and praising God and the Lamb. Even if we *could* go to heaven with the gratification of our lusts, we should prefer a way of holiness and conformity to the spiritual self-denying rules of the gospel.

It's one thing to live one's life in a manner pleasing to Christ. It's another to cast aside everything that takes our eyes from Him so that our path is cleared before us. Sometimes my path is pretty cluttered.

However, there are moments—supreme moments—when I experience a sort of heavenly communion with the saints above. These moments happen sometimes when I pray. Most of the time they occur during worship.

At church, our worship pastor frequently reminds us that, for the brief interval of time when we're singing great songs of praise and adoration together, we are joining our voices to the heavenly voices who sing God's praise without ceasing. It's when music combines with absolute truth and praise that I sense that truest worship—and never want it to stop.

Someday I'll have that and more—not for a few brief minutes, but for eternity. Maybe this glimpse of glory is what Edwards is writing about here.

John Piper wrote, "What Edwards saw in God and in the universe because of God, through the lens of

Scripture, was breathtaking."[2] Yearning for that as we live daily is what Jonathan Edwards is urging us towards.

3. We should travel on in this way in a laborious manner.—Long journeys are attended with toil and fatigue, especially if through a wilderness. Persons in such a case expect no other than to suffer hardships and weariness.—So we should travel in this way of holiness, improving our time and strength, to surmount the difficulties and obstacles that are in the way. The land we have to travel through, is a wilderness. There are many mountains, rocks, and rough places that we must go over, and therefore there is a necessity that we should lay out our strength.

4. Our whole lives ought to be spent in traveling this road.—We ought to be *early.* This should be the *first* concern, when persons become capable of acting. When they first set out in the *world,* they should set out on *this* journey.—And we ought to travel on with *assiduity.* It ought to be the work of every day. We should often think of our journey's end; and make it our daily work to travel on in the way that leads to it.—He who is on a journey is often thinking of the destined place, and it is his daily care and business to get along and to improve his time to get towards his journey's end. Thus should heaven be continually in our thoughts. And the immediate entrance or passage to it, *viz.* death, should be present with us.—We ought to *persevere* in this way as long as we live.

"Let us run with patience the race that is

---

2.   John Piper and Justin Taylor, eds., *A God Entranced Vision of All Things: The Legacy of Jonathan Edwards* (Wheaton, IL: Crossway, 2004). p22.

set before us." (Heb. 12:1) Though the road be difficult and toilsome, we must hold out with patience, and be content to endure hardships. Though the journey be long, yet we must not stop short, but hold on till we arrive at the place we seek. Nor should we be discouraged with the length and difficulties of the way, as the children of Israel were, and be for turning back again. All our thought and design should be to press forward till we arrive.

Travel can be a joyful experience, but it can also be tedious, exhausting, frustrating and frightening. I think of long layovers in airports, or of trying to catch a connecting flight with seconds to spare. I think of lost luggage, of ruined schedules of sleeping, eating, and bathing. I think of blisters on my feet, of hunger and thirst. I think of people who set up camp next to me in the airport and want to talk my ear off about nothing.

Yet even in the nicest airports, it's just a stop along the way. Your heart is still set upon the final destination, isn't it?

I used to travel to meet a friend for a week in some locale neither of us had been before. Since I only saw her once or twice a year it was always a treat. Knowing she was on the other end of my travels made me impatient to get there. I couldn't wait for us to be reunited again. It never mattered how nice my airport experience was—I was always anxious to get to the destination.

Yes, it was possible to enjoy things along the way, but my eyes and my heart were focused on the final destination. That's how I see what Edwards is saying.

In my analogy, it was the reunion with a friend that drew me. In Edwards' sermon, it's Christ who draws our strongest yearning.

We know what it's like to journey on this life pilgrimage with Him spiritually. There, we will finally be able to see Him in the fullness of His glory. That reunion becomes the impetus for our fervent forward movement toward heaven in this life. What joy awaits us there.

5.   We ought to be continually growing in holiness, and in that respect coming nearer and nearer to heaven—We should be endeavoring to come nearer to heaven, in being more heavenly, becoming more and more like the inhabitants of heaven in respect of holiness and conformity to God, the knowledge of God and Christ, in clear views of the glory of God, the beauty of Christ, and the excellency of divine things, as we come nearer to the beatific vision.—We should labor to be continually growing in divine love—that this may be an increasing flame in our hearts, till they ascend wholly in this flame—in obedience and a heavenly conversation, that we may do the will of God on earth as the angels do in heaven, in comfort and spiritual joy, [and] in sensible communion with God and Jesus Christ. Our path should be as "the shining light, that shines more and more to the perfect day." (Pro. 4:18) We ought to be hungering and thirsting after righteousness; after an increase in righteousness. "As new-born babes, desire the sincere milk of the word, that ye may grow thereby." (1 Pet. 2:2) The perfection of heaven should be our mark. "This one thing I do, forgetting those things which are behind, and

> reaching forth unto those things that are before,
> I press toward the mark, for the prize of the high
> calling God in Christ Jesus." (Phil. 3:13-14)

Lest you think this is just Jonathan Edwards' mindset, let me ask you to reread the passages he quotes along the way. No, it is not some kind of religious fanaticism that produces his godly direction to us. He derives his principles from Scripture!

This is what the Apostle Paul advocated and taught in these passages. This is what the Apostle Peter told us when he said we are to live with our eyes focused upon heavenly things.

Yes, we are instructed in the Bible to seek first the kingdom of God. We are instructed to become more Christlike. We are encouraged to work toward greater sanctification.

As we move along that ascending trajectory that reflects our sanctification, we become more and more like Christ. "For those whom he foreknew he also predestined to be conformed to the image of his Son," (Rom. 8:29).

"Do not be conformed to this world, but be transformed by the renewal of your mind," (Rom 12:2).

That's what our lives are all about—being transformed into Christlikeness. And we do it by renewing our minds. Being in the Scriptures daily is of vital importance. The more time we spend in God's Word, the more we will be transformed into Christ's likeness—to adopt His principles, His values, His characteristics, His adoration for the Father.

Minds marinated in the truths of God's Word result in changed behaviors, changed patterns of thought.

Bible intake comes in many forms—hearing, reading, studying, memorizing and meditation (prolonged thinking).

Don Whitney writes, "Reading is the exposure to Scripture—and that's the starting place—but meditation is the absorption of Scripture that causes the water of the word of God to percolate deeply into the parched soil of the soul and refresh it." [3]

These disciplines are essential in our sanctification, the process by which we become more and more Christlike. Our intimacy with Him produces this growth in spiritual maturity.

We may not be able to attain Jonathan Edwards' mental acumen. However, we can incorporate his disciplines of prayer and various means of Bible intake into our lives.

John Piper wrote about this. "The spiritual disciplines are the practical ways whereby we obey the command of 1 Timothy 4:7-8." [4] "Have nothing to do with irreverent, silly myths. Rather train yourself for godliness: for while bodily training is of some value, godliness is of value in every way, as it holds promise for the present life and also for the life to come." The goal is godliness. Spiritual disciplines move us forward to that goal.

> 6. All other concerns of life ought to be entirely subordinate to this.—When a man is on a journey, all the steps he takes are subordinated to the aim of getting to his journey's end. And if he carries money or provisions with him, it is to supply him in his journey. So we ought wholly

---

3.　Ibid. p. 112, 44.
4.　Ibid. p. 110.

> to subordinate all our other business, and all our temporal enjoyments, to this affair of traveling to heaven. When anything we have becomes a clog and hindrance to us, we should quit it immediately. The use of our worldly enjoyments and possessions, should be with such a view, and in such a manner, as to further us in our way heavenward. Thus we should eat, and drink, and clothe ourselves, and improve the conversation and enjoyment of friends. And whatever business we are setting about, whatever design we are engaging in, we should inquire with ourselves, whether this business or undertaking will forward us in our way to heaven? And if not, we should quit our design."

Buckle your seat belts. Prepare for takeoff.

We're all on a journey. Whether our journey is long or short, level or steep, smooth or rocky, we are to incorporate these godly principles into our daily walk.

Not to Jonathan Edwards' level of maturity yet? Pray to that end. Ask the Lord to give you maturity, to bless your reading of Scripture, to plant His principles deeply into your soul, to equip you with everything you'll require to reach the place where you can begin to yearn to be clothed with our heavenly dwelling.

I've heard it said, "Don't be so heavenly-minded you're of no earthly good." Edwards is not saying our earthly lives should be shunned as we press onward towards heaven. He was of great earthly good during his journey.

He was a child prodigy, entering Yale University at the age of twelve, and reigned there as head of the class, obtaining his master's degree before he was out of his teens, accepting his first pastorate in his late teens, then preaching, teaching, pastoring for the rest of his life. He is considered by many to be this country's greatest scholar and theologian.

Not only that, but he was deeply in love with his wife, Sarah, and together they produced eleven children. His home life was rich, loving and meaningful and he taught his children to honor God with their lives. He had great friends and participated in life's enjoyments— while never taking his eyes off the prize.

He would advocate being a responsible member of society, that we should engage in good deeds, that we should enjoy good things, that we should continue to know and teach the Scriptures, that we are to live productive lives for Christ, that we are to provide for and love our families and be a joy to all who know us. What he warns against is that while you're doing these things, do not see them as an end to themselves. We are not to rest in any of this. Our rest is yet to come—it is to be found in our heavenly eternity.

*****

Questions for Reflection

1. What does it mean to "live with the end in sight?"
2. How does an exuberant joy in heavenly things protect you from sorrow and pain in your earthly life?
3. Explain the concept of being foreigners, strangers, aliens in this life. Where is our true home/country?
4. What does it mean to be "set apart?"
5. Which analogy brought greater clarity to *your* thinking? Can you think of others?
   - Traveling along a steep hill of obstacles and difficulty?
   - Our lives represented by a pilgrimage toward a final destination?
   - Waiting in an airport?
   - Going on a vacation with a joyful destination awaiting us?

CHAPTER TWO

SECTION II

Why the Christian's life is a journey, or pilgrimage?

1. This world is not our abiding place. Our continuance
    here is but very short. Man's days on the earth,
    are as a shadow. It was never designed by God
    that this world should be our home. Neither did
    God give us these temporal accommodations for
    that end. If God has given us ample estates, and
    children, or other pleasant friends, it is with no
    such design, that we should be furnished here,
    as for a settled abode, but with a design that we
    should use them for the present, and then leave
    them in a very little time. When we are called to
    any secular business, or charged with the care
    of a family, [and] if we improve our lives to any
    other purpose than as a journey toward heaven,
    all our labor will be lost. If we spend our lives in
    the pursuit of a temporal happiness, as riches or
    sensual pleasures, credit and esteem from men,
    delight in our children and the prospect of seeing
    them well brought up and well settled, etc.—all
    these things will be of little significancy to us.
    Death will blow up all our hopes, and will put an
    end to these enjoyments. "The places that have
    known us, will know us no more" and "the eye that

> has seen us, shall see us no more." We must be
> taken away forever from all these things, and it is
> uncertain when: it may be soon after we are put
> into the possession of them. And then, where will
> be all our worldly employments and enjoyments,
> when we are laid in the silent grave! "So man lieth
> down, and riseth not again, till the heavens be no
> more." (Job 14:12)

At nearly every funeral I attend, I hear someone say, "He was only on loan to us." Very true. We're all "on loan" in this foreign country where we live. Everything we're given here is merely on loan, designed for our use and enjoyment—blessings but not treasures we set our hearts upon.

Our lives are so brief. As James says, "What is your life? For you are a mist that appears for a little time and then vanishes," (Jas. 4:14).

When I read through Genesis, I see phrases that say that so and so lived so many years and then they died. Again and again, I read this. When I read Stephen's recounting of Old Testament history in Acts 7, I see the continuous flow of history as one man was raised to leadership and another rose to take his place. It's this beautiful continuity that strikes me when considering the number of years during which this takes place and the events, situations, details and individuals we're told of throughout that history. And it all works within God's divine master plan.

I realize that for even the greatest men, like Moses or David, their lives were like a mist which appeared and then disappeared in the huge scheme of things. So what about us "little people" in the grand scheme? We make a difference. Yes. But, like Moses and David, when we have accomplished all He has called us to do, it's time for us to leave, to escape these earthly bodies we inhabit and flee instantly to Christ's side.

In light of this, we need to be busy about living lives for Christ—responsible lives according to biblical principles, loving others, and doing the good He ordains for each of us. Our deaths are not in our hands. God determines our length of days. Psalm 139:16 explains that all the days ordained for us were numbered before even one of them came to be. We are not to concern ourselves with that.

When Jesus told Peter the manner of death to expect, Peter immediately asked, "Well, what about him [meaning John]?" And Jesus told him, "If it is my will that he remain until I come, what is that to you? You follow me!" (John 21:22). In this light rebuke, Jesus refocuses Peter on the task at hand—on the bottom line.

He's saying, "Don't worry about John's life—or your own. What you need to concentrate upon is one thing—following Me." When it comes right down to it, isn't that what we're all to do? Isn't that what this life is for? We follow Him imperfectly here, but we'll follow Him perfectly when we reach the other side.

That's why we're not to focus so much on this world we live in, on the possessions He's given us, or on the families and friends we're a part of. Edwards repeatedly advises us to be ready to leave everything behind when our time comes to depart—and to do it joyfully. Sometimes death comes at the end of an illness. Other times it happens suddenly and without any warning.

Either way, believers are to live anticipating our glorious life to come—we should be prepared and ready to go when our Father calls.

God gives some people long lives, like my father's eighty-eight years. Others are very short—some only a few brief minutes. But everything they were to accomplish was fulfilled. Their birth and death, their very existence no matter how long or how brief, accomplishes something. In those few moments, people's lives are changed.

Like those in Hebrews' Hall of Faith, some people never get to see the promise of their goals fulfilled. I recently heard of someone who graduated from college with honors—something that requires an enormous amount of work. They graduated last month and died this month of Covid-19. Then there's the fellow who worked hard his entire life and looked forward to retirement. He already had plans to travel, to update his house and visit his children and grandchildren. And he died three months into his retirement.

In each case, everything those individuals were meant by God to accomplish was fulfilled. In our eyes, these situations may seem unfair and tragic. Not so with God. His sovereign design is perfect—even though we may not be able to see it right now. It's not about us. The bottom line is that everything is always about Him.

Edwards understood this. He believed that God is the beginning, the middle and the end of all things.

Life and death are uncertain. But we are to focus on following Christ.

Yes, God gave us spectacular blessings to enjoy while we're here. It is God-honoring to give him thanks and praise for His provisions. But we're not to get too comfortable. He didn't put us here for that.

Edwards believed that when God saves us, the greatest blessing He gives us is the gift of . . . Himself. That was the source of Edwards' joy.

So why did He leave us here? He could have zapped us into heaven the instant we believed in Him. He didn't. That wasn't His plan. Only one answer suffices. We are to be busy about the works of righteousness He has already planned for us—and those works are different for each of us. Our lives are to be a witness for and to Him.

What about your life? Do you adorn Him? Or do you defame Him? He created us. He saved us. Now we are to accomplish what He put us here for as we journey home to Him.

"For we are his workmanship, created in Christ Jesus for good works, which God prepared beforehand, that we should walk in them," (Eph. 2:10). Every good purpose God intends us to perform on earth will be accomplished by the time we reach our heavenly dwelling.

How do I know that? Because of HIM! He planned these earthly works in advance. He, through the Holy Spirit, equips us to will and to do the things He has planned for us. His will cannot be thwarted. Therefore, we will do them as directed.

Every good thing we do is because the Father planned it. We carry it out—it seems like our idea. But that's because the Holy Spirit directs our hearts to do the will of God. Because of that, we really cannot take any of the credit for the good we do, yet because of the kindness and grace of God, He credits us with it anyway.

Yes, being in the family of God is a joyful, joyful state.

2. The future world was designed to be our settled and everlasting abode. There it was intended that we should be fixed, and there alone is a lasting habitation and a lasting inheritance. The present state is short and transitory, but our state in the other world is everlasting. And as we are there at first, so we must be without change. Our state in the future world, therefore, being eternal, is of so much greater importance than our state here, that all our concerns in this world should be wholly subordinated to it.

3. Heaven is that place alone where our highest end and highest good is to be obtained. God hath made us for himself. "Of him, and through him, and to him are all things." Therefore, then do we attain to our highest end, when we are brought to God: but that is by being brought to heaven, for that is God's throne, the place of his special presence. There is but a very imperfect union with God to be had in this world, a very imperfect knowledge of him in the midst of much darkness: a very imperfect conformity to God, mingled with abundance of estrangement. Here we can serve and glorify God, but in a very imperfect manner: our service being mingled with sin, which dishonors God—But when we get to heaven (if ever that be), we shall be brought to a perfect union with God and have more clear views of him. There we shall be fully conformed to God, without any remaining sin: for "we shall see him as he is."

There we shall serve God perfectly and glorify him in an exalted manner, even to the utmost of the powers and capacity of our nature. Then we shall perfectly give up ourselves to God: our hearts will be pure and holy offerings, presented in a flame of divine love.

God is the highest good of the reasonable creature, and the enjoyment of him is the only happiness with which our souls can be satisfied.— To go to heaven fully to enjoy God, is *infinitely* better than the most pleasant accommodations here. Fathers and mothers, husbands, wives, children, or the company of earthly friends, are but shadows. But the enjoyment of God is the substance. These are but scattered beams, but God is the sun. These are but streams, but God is the fountain. These are but drops, but God is the ocean.—Therefore it becomes us to spend this life only as a journey towards heaven, as it becomes us to make the seeking of our highest end and proper good, the whole work of our lives, to which we should subordinate all other concerns of life. Why should we labor for, or set our hearts on anything else, but that which is our proper end, and true happiness?

I think about this often. When I look over God's creation, our natural world, I cannot imagine anything more beautiful. Yes, I know we're told this world is but a shadow compared to the world to come. I'm only saying my mind is too inadequate to imagine anything more exquisite than what He's already created.

I enjoyed Edwards' comparisons in this point:

- Fathers and mothers, husbands, wives, children, or the company of earthly friends, are but shadows. The enjoyment of God is the substance.
- These are but scattered beams, but God is the sun.
- These are but streams, but God is the fountain.
- These are but drops, but God is the ocean.

It reminds me of the book of Hebrews which deals with the supremacy of Christ in all things. Here we see the supremacy of God as it relates even to our enjoyment of the world He created.

Edwards understood this. Nature drew him like a magnet. One of his favorite activities was riding horseback along the Hudson River to sit under a tree outside town and meditate upon God's power and artistry displayed in the beauty of His creation.

It was common for him to sit and meditate upon the sky as storm clouds gathered and to watch them move closer. He loved storms. He loved nature.

In this point of his sermon, I believe Edwards is reminding us that even our most pleasurable experiences, our most intense enjoyments here are nothing compared to what we will experience in that true fellowship with our Lord. We only think we can comprehend joy in the here and now.

Again, I admit to my own limitations when I say I cannot imagine this kind of pure joy in the Lord. I get the impression that Edwards could.

4. Our present state, and all that belongs to it, is designed by him that made all things, to be wholly in order to another world.—This world was made for a place of preparation for another.

Man's mortal life was given him, that he might be prepared for his fixed state. And all that God has here given us, is given to this purpose. The sun shines, the rain falls upon us, and the earth yields her increase to us for this end. Civil, ecclesiastical, and family affairs, and all our personal concerns, are designed and ordered in subordination to a future world, by the maker and disposer of all things. To this therefore they ought to be subordinated by us.

It's all about God. It was all about God in the beginning, through all the courses of history, and will be in the end, as well. This wonderful world He has given us is nothing compared to what He is planning for our future.

What we need to focus upon is following Him. He's already taken care of the rest.

*****

Questions for Reflection

1. What are the most significant things we can accomplish on earth in terms of our heavenly destination?
2. Our lives are but a mist, a vapor, according to James. So what ultimate value do our lives have on earth?
3. Why is it futile to wring our hands about the day of our death if we belong to Christ?
4. Edwards says that *nothing* we experience here will hold a candle to the joy that awaits us in heaven. What are some of the comparisons he uses to convey this?
5. At the bottom line, what is to be our main concern in life? (This is what Jesus told Peter in John 21.)

CHAPTER THREE

SECTION III

Instruction afforded by the consideration, that life is a journey or pilgrimage, towards heaven.

1. This doctrine may teach us moderation in our mourning for the loss of such dear friends, who while they lived, improved their lives to right purposes. If they lived a holy life, then their lives were a journey towards heaven. And why should we be immoderate in mourning, when they are got to their journey's end? Death, though it appears to us with a frightful aspect, is to them a great blessing. Their end is happy, and better than their beginning. "The day of their death, is better than the day of their birth." (Ecc. 7:1) While they lived, they desired heaven, and chose it above this world or any of its enjoyments. For this they earnestly longed, and why should we grieve that they have obtained it?—Now they have got to their Father's house. They find more comfort a thousand times now they are gone home, than they did in their journey. In this world they underwent much labor and toil: it was a wilderness they passed through. There were many difficulties in the way: mountains and rough places. It was laborious and fatiguing to travel the road, and they had many

wearisome days and nights: but now they have got to their everlasting rest. "And I heard a voice from heaven, saying unto me, Write, blessed are the dead which die in the Lord from henceforth: yea, saith the Spirit, that they may rest from their labors; and their works do follow them." (Rev. 14:13) They look back upon the difficulties, and sorrows, and dangers of life, rejoicing that they have surmounted them all.

We are ready to look upon death as their calamity, and to mourn that those who were so dear to us should be in the dark grave: that they are there transformed to corruption and worms, taken away from their dear children and enjoyments, etc. as though they were in awful circumstances. But this is owing to our infirmity. They are in a happy condition, inconceivably blessed. They do not mourn, but rejoice with exceeding joy: their mouths are filled with joyful songs, and they drink at rivers of pleasure. They find no mixture of grief that they have changed their earthly enjoyments, and the company of mortals, for heaven. Their life here, though in the best circumstances, was attended with much that was adverse and afflictive, but now there is an end to all adversity. "They shall hunger no more nor thirst any more; neither shall the sun light on them, nor any heat. For the Lamb which is in the midst of the throne, shall feed them and shall lead them unto living fountains of waters: and God shall wipe away all tears from their eyes." (Rev. 7:16-17)

It is true, we shall see them no more in this world, yet we ought to consider that we are traveling towards the same place; and why should we break our hearts that they have got there before us? We are following after them, and hope as soon as we get to our journey's end to be with them again, in better circumstances. A degree of mourning for near relations when departed is not inconsistent with Christianity, but very agreeable to it. For as long as we are flesh and blood, we have animal propensities and affections. But we have just reason that our mourning should be mingled with joy. "But I would not have you to be ignorant, brethren, concerning them that are asleep, that ye sorrow not, even as others that have no hope." (1 Thes. 4:13) i.e. that they should not sorrow as the heathen, who had no knowledge of a future happiness. This appears by the following verse; "for if we believe that Jesus died and rose again, even so them also which sleep in Jesus, will God bring with him."

I thank the Lord that my father was a Christian because that was my consolation as he lay dying. Along the way, I'd tell him, "Just think, Daddy. In a little while you'll be in heaven face-to-face with Jesus. What a joy that will be." I held his hand, I sang to him, I prayed for him, I cared for him and talked to him—all to remind him of the beauty he was about to encounter and encourage him as he neared the finish line.

Remembering it brings tears to my eyes even now. But as Edwards here instructs us, I realize that we grieve, not for our loved one, but for ourselves—and for that part of us we lose as a result.

My relationship with my father was different from any other relationship in my world. Who I was with him, I will be with no one else. In that sense, that part of me died, too. I'll miss it. And I'll miss him and the certain brand of sweetness and integrity he brought to this world.

But my pain is due to my loss. When I think of my father, I do not picture his body in the grave. His body was not him. No, he spent the last fifty-five years trapped in a body that steadily descended into helplessness—becoming blind, almost completely deaf, and with dementia that finally became so severe that he became dependent on others for all of his needs. But now. What glorious words! But now he sees clearly, hears perfectly, moves freely and his mind is sharp so he can experience all the glories of heaven. His death is truly better than his life.

Edwards certainly would understand both my pain and my joy at my father's passing. He taught us in this sermon that we shouldn't feel sorry for the believer who has passed into glory.

D. L. Moody reflected this in his famous words. "Some day you will read in the papers, 'D. L. Moody of East Northfield is dead.' Don't you believe a word of it! At that moment I shall be more alive than I am now."

It wouldn't surprise me if he had read this sermon himself! Obviously, D. L. Moody comprehended the truth of it, and lived his life with the end in sight.

Let's go back to the airport analogy. When I traveled with my friend, we'd ride to the airport together on our way home. If her flight to Austin was at 12:40 and mine to Little Rock wasn't until 1:10, I was happy for her. She would make it home before me. Yeah, I'd miss her presence after she left, but it was a good thing that her flight left first.

In the same way, when we lose a loved one, their "flight" merely took off before ours. We are to be happy for them—not feel sorry for them. Several of my loved ones have preceded me to heaven, and it gives me pleasure to think of them there. Even if I could, I wouldn't bring them back here for anything.

2. If our lives ought to be only a journey towards heaven, how ill do they improve their lives, that spend them in traveling towards hell?—Some men spend their whole lives, from their infancy to their dying day, in going down the broad way to destruction. They not only draw nearer to hell as to time, but they every day grow more ripe for destruction. They are more assimilated to the inhabitants of the internal world. While others press forward in the straight and narrow way to life and laboriously travel up the hill toward Zion, against the inclinations and tendency of the flesh, these run with a swift career down to eternal death. This is the employment of every day, with all wicked men, and the whole day is spent in it. As soon as ever they awake in the morning, they set out anew in the way to hell and spend every waking moment in it. They begin in early days. "The wicked are estranged from the womb, they go astray as soon as they are born, speaking lies." (Psa. 58:3) They hold on it with perseverance. Many of them who live to be old, are never weary in it. Though they live to be an hundred years old, they will not cease traveling in the way to hell till they arrive there. And all the concerns of life are subordinated to this employment. A wicked man is a servant of sin, his powers and faculties are employed in the service of sin and in fitness for

hell. And all his possessions are so used by him as to be subservient to the same purpose. Men spend their time in treasuring up wrath against the day of wrath. Thus do all unclean persons, who live in lascivious practices in secret: all malicious persons, all profane persons that neglect the duties of religion. Thus do all unjust persons, and those who are fraudulent and oppressive in their dealings. Thus do all backbiters and revilers, all covetous persons that set their hearts chiefly on the riches of this world. Thus do tavern-haunters, and frequenters of evil company, and many other kinds that might be mentioned. Thus the bulk of mankind are hastening onward in the broad way to destruction, which is, as it were, filled up with the multitude that are going in it with one accord. And they are every day going to hell out of this broad way by thousands. Multitudes are continually flowing down into the great lake of fire and brimstone, as some mighty river constantly disembogues its water into the ocean.

First of all, "disembogues" means to empty or discharge a stream or smaller river into the sea or into a larger river. That's probably not a word you hear every day.

Yes, this is the same Jonathan Edwards who preached his most famous sermon, "Sinners in the Hands of an Angry God." And yes, he is criticized for his graphic fire and brimstone illustrations in that sermon. People paint Edwards with a brush that colors him harsh, cold, unfeeling, judgmental, morose and dark. That couldn't be farther from the truth.

Many say that Jonathan Edwards was the most brilliant man this country ever produced. His life was characterized by joy, not anger. He believed in loving and serving others, and in keeping his love for God primary in every aspect of his life.

I've read that Edwards had an overwhelming sense of the beauty of Christ, the intimacy of the Holy Spirit, and God's glory and majesty. Yet, he also clearly saw God's wrath and judgment, punishment and justice as other parts of His divine nature.

Is God's wrath on display in "Sinners in the Hands of an Angry God'? Yes, but God's mercy was also described. People seem to remember the negative.

Even his stern language emerged from a heart that had such a love for the lost that he wanted to get their attention any way he could. Even if it gave the impression of being harsh and vengeful, it was intended to make people think rightly about God and to lead to salvation for the lost.

You see a little of the same language in this section of the sermon. One tiny criticism I offer is that it reads as if sinners consciously seek hell, that they rush headlong into it with full volition. I do not think that is the case (and I'm sure he didn't either).

Sinners do not seek to go to hell. It happens as a result of their life. Christians go to heaven because they live their lives serving Christ, believing in Him, following Him, worshiping Him. Sinners go to hell because they live their lives serving self, following their own standards, doing what seems right in their own eyes—all of them involved in some form of self-worship (egocentricity). What they think, do or say is governed by their own standards of right and wrong—much more relevant and important to them than the Word of God.

Their god is their own happiness and satisfaction. Edwards preached that happiness wasn't the result of self-fulfillment. Instead, he urged them to "God-contentedness." That can only be achieved through unshakable dependence upon Him.

Edwards passionately appeals to them, pleading with them to turn from their own sin and love of self to a belief in the one true God and Jesus Christ, His Son. Love motivates his plea. He didn't want to think of anyone going to hell—especially if there was anything he could do to prevent it.

In fact, Edwards was a primary player in the Great Awakening in this country in the late 1730s and early 1740s. With his preaching, and George Whitefield's revival efforts in New England, a great revival occurred. God used these men in boundless ways and many people were saved as a result of their work.

So before you read a section like this one and label Jonathan Edwards as one of those unforgiving, unloving, strict Puritans, please do not miss the rest of the sermon which deals with the absolute joy produced by the existence and glory of Almighty God.

3. Hence when persons are converted they do but begin their work and set out in the way they have to go.—They never till then do anything at that work in which their whole lives ought to be spent. Persons before conversion never take a step that way. Then does a man first set out on his journey, when he is brought home to Christ, and so far is he from having done his work, that his care and labor in his Christian work and business, is then but begun, in which he must spend the remaining part of his life.

Those persons do ill, who when they are converted and have obtained a hope of their being in a good condition, do not strive as earnestly as they did before, while they were under awakenings. They ought, henceforward, as long as they live, to be as earnest and laborious, as watchful and careful as ever: yea, they should increase more and more. It is no just excuse that now they have obtained conversion. Should not we be as diligent as that we ourselves may be that we may serve and glorify God, happy? And if we have obtained grace, yet we ought to strive as much that we may obtain the other degrees that are before, as we did to obtain that small degree that is behind. The apostle tells us that he forgot what was behind and reached forth towards what was before. (Phil. 3:13)

Yea, those who are converted have now a further reason to strive for grace. For they have seen something of its excellency. A man who has once tasted the blessing of Canaan, has more reason to press towards it than he had before. And they who are converted, should strive to "make their calling and election sure." All those who are converted are not sure of it, and those who are sure, do not know that they shall be always so, and still, seeking and serving God with the utmost diligence, is the way to have assurance and to have it maintained.

Here he adopts the Apostle Paul's device, the one he used when writing to the Thessalonians—something like: Yes, you're a model for the world, now do so more and more. Yes, you love your brothers in an exemplary fashion, now do so more and more.

57

Edwards takes the sinner saved by grace and says, in essence, "it's such a great and momentous thing that you've turned to embrace Jesus as your Lord and Savior, but now is not the time to lie down and rest. Now is the call to action. Be busy about making your calling and election sure. Let the rest of your life focus on following Christ by implementing the biblical principles He gave us through His Word, by loving and serving others, and by glorifying the King of Heaven."

Our devotion to Christ should be reflected in every area of our lives—financial, social, marital, religious, intellectual and spiritual. To Him, everything is related because everything is related to God. No area of life should lie outside that biblical influence. That's what living for Christ is about. Doing in each area of life what would please our Savior.

He is our master. Every waking hour should be spent doing what serves Him best—whether in our relationships with others, in our service, in our ministry, in our employment, or in our enjoyment of life itself. Paul says it best, in Romans 12:1: "I appeal to you therefore, brothers, by the mercies of God, to present your bodies as a living sacrifice, holy and acceptable to God, which is your spiritual worship."

Living sacrifices. Every day devoted to Him. Extreme? Some would think so. Jonathan Edwards would not. He is one of our greatest examples of presenting his life as a living sacrifice to Christ, his Savior. Perhaps, as mentioned before, we can't attain to his level of knowledge and obedience. He sets the bar high and we strive toward it. The blessing is in the striving.

*****

Questions for Reflection

1. Think of the most recent loss of a loved one. If that individual was a believer, meditate upon what his/her life may be like in heaven. Ask yourself, "If it were possible, would I want to bring them back to this world?" Why? Or Why not?

2. How is it possible to feel so much joy for your loved one, yet so much pain in your own heart when you consider losing them?

3. Do you think your deceased loved ones are watching over you? (I've heard that from many families who've lost loved ones.) Put yourself in their shoes for a moment: face-to-face with Jesus, experiencing His glory, bathed in heavenly joy and more pure love than they've ever known. If that were you, would you care what was going on in the world beneath you?

4. Part of living a life with the end in sight is warning others about what lies ahead. Picture standing in a torrential downpour as a car races toward you. The occupants of the car don't know the bridge ahead is out and they're speeding toward a certain death. Do you let them go past to their own peril or do you try to wave your arms and get them to stop, to see the danger ahead and turn around while they can? How is that any different from what Jonathan Edwards (and every true believer) does?

5. Complacency is not a word that should be applied to a Christian. We are to continue to love and grow and learn and flourish. In what ways are you striving to move forward in your Christian journey?

CHAPTER FOUR

SECTION IV

An exhortation so to spend the present life, that it may only be a journey towards heaven

Labor to obtain such a disposition of mind that you may choose heaven for your inheritance and home, and may earnestly long for it and be willing to change this world, and all its enjoyments, for heaven. Labor to have your heart taken up so much about heaven, and heavenly enjoyments, as that you may rejoice when God calls you to leave your best earthly friends and comforts for heaven, there to enjoy God and Christ.

Be persuaded to travel in the way that leads to heaven: *viz.* in holiness, self-denial, mortification, obedience to all the commands of God, following Christ's example in a way of heavenly life, or imitation of the saints and angels in heaven. Let it be your daily work, from morning till night, and hold out in it to the end. Let nothing stop or discourage you, or turn you aside from this road. And let all other concerns be subordinated to this. Consider the reasons that have been mentioned why you should thus spend your life: that this world is not your abiding place, that the future world is to be your everlasting abode, and that the enjoyments and concerns of this world are given entirely in order to another. And consider further for motive.

1. How worthy is heaven that your life should be wholly spent as a journey towards it.—To what better purpose can you spend your life, whether you respect your duty or your interest? What better end can you propose to your journey, than to obtain heaven? You are placed in this world with a choice given you, that you may travel which way you please, and one way leads to heaven. Now, can you direct your course better than this way? All men have some aim or other in living. Some mainly seek worldly things. They spend their days in such pursuits. But is not heaven, where is fullness of joy forever, much more worthy to be sought by you? How can you better employ your strength, use your means, and spend your days, than in traveling the road that leads to the everlasting enjoyment of God: to his glorious presence, to the new Jerusalem, to the heavenly mount Zion, where all your desires will be filled and no danger of ever losing your happiness?—No man is at home in this world, whether he choose heaven or not: here he is but a transient person. Where can you choose your home better than in heaven?

Is Jonathan Edwards saying that we need to do nothing but spend our days working for the Lord? Are we to set up a stepstool on a corner and preach all day, every day? Or abandon all relationships in life to become monk-like as we study the Bible? Or to never have a moment for relaxation or enjoyment? No, he is not saying that.

It's true that some spend almost their every waking hour about the ministry of Christ. Many of those are pastors, teachers, missionaries—you know, professionals.

However, I don't think that's what he's talking about. He never says we can't work to provide for our families, or do the kinds of things it takes to run a busy household. He doesn't say we can't have other interests. He doesn't say we can't gather in groups to fellowship with one another, or engage in celebration, or enjoy good food, or to enjoy the world of things He created for us.

I believe he's saying that we are to keep our focus on following Christ as we go about our lives. What does that mean? It means that we don't do anything contrary to His will. It means that we live as Christians in this world—as representatives of Christ. And that we represent Him well.

That involves how we conduct ourselves, how we treat other people, how we speak, and what we talk about, how we thank God for all things and never take anything for granted, and about how we press forward in our walk with the Lord.

Where is our focus? Where is our treasure? Worldly things? Or godly things? We should not "forsake the assembling of ourselves together' in His Name. We should be lifelong students of the Scriptures. We should be willing and ready, in season and out, to speak about spiritual issues. We should keep ourselves pure and avoid all manner of sexual immorality. Our love for the lost should motivate us to speak to them about salvation through Christ.

Yet we must be practical here. Most of us do not have the opportunity to devote ourselves to study and prayer thirteen hours a day, like Edwards did. Most of us have to work, to manage households, to raise children, and to stick with busy schedules. Could we find more time to spend with the Lord in study and prayer? Certainly. I want to challenge both myself and you to do so.

Yet, I understand that our individual lives dictate how much time we have for this. Besides, none of us should close ourselves off from people to live as a hermit. How can we practice love for others unless we are actually with them?

That's why I say that it's entirely possible to live your lives with the end in sight by:

- following the principles of Christ,
- studying His Word,
- glorifying Him in all things,
- spending time with Him often in prayer,
- and reflecting Him in all our relationships and the roles He places us in.

We live with heaven as our final destination and our lives are to reflect that. We do it as we live our lives, ever mindful of the Lord in every aspect of life.

No longer do we value things or people or status or power or riches more than our relationship with Christ. No longer do we lay up treasure on earth but instead we lay up treasure in heaven. That way we do not depend on any earthly thing as the source of our joy.

Instead, our joy is wrapped up in what cannot be destroyed, on what cannot diminish, on what does not perish. Then, no matter what we encounter upon our journey through life, we will not be abandoned to despair or bewilderment or even sorrow.

Because of the hope of heaven, we will live our lives in hopeful expectation. If we are securely tethered to Jesus, nothing can take away our ultimate joy.

When "God is at the center, the self is most realized, most fulfilled, and most happy."[1] Edwards' life reflected this. For Jonathan Edwards, his joy derived from knowing God. He was so entranced with God that his life was consumed with Him.

Let us all be more consumed with God, and we may also experience the kind of joy that cannot be destroyed.

> 2. This is the way to have death comfortable to us.— To spend our lives so as to be only a journeying towards heaven, is the way to be free from bondage and to have the prospect and forethought of death comfortable. Does the traveler think of his journey's end? Were the children of Israel sorry after forty years' travel in the wilderness, when they had almost got to Canaan? This is the way to be able to part with the world without grief. Does it grieve the traveler when he has got home, to quit his staff and load of provisions that he had to sustain him by the way?

Ever been on a long vacation with a lot of travel, days spent going to one attraction after another, following an itinerary, eating and sleeping at odd times? No matter how great the trip was, what do you feel the moment you pull into your driveway, walk into your home, and drop your bags?

---

1. Ibid, p. 52.

Ahhhh. That's the kind of relief that awaits us. Will we miss the journey once we've arrived at our final destination? Heavens, no!

No matter how enjoyable that vacation was to us, it's always sweet to collapse into your old recliner or comfortable bed and return to your own sense of "being home." There's really no place like home, is there?

Our heavenly home is like that. We are transient until we get there. But once there, the bliss and sweet enjoyment of home will eclipse anything we've experienced here on earth.

3. No more of your life will be pleasant to think of when you come to die, than has been spent after this manner.—If you have spent none of your life this way, your whole life will be terrible to you to think of, unless you die under some great delusion. You will see then, that all of your life that has been spent otherwise, is lost. You will then see the vanity of all other aims that you may have proposed to yourself. The thought of what you here possessed and enjoyed will not be pleasant to you, unless you can think also that you have subordinated them to this purpose.

I call this his "wood, hay and straw" point. Everything he writes is grounded in Scripture, but this one comes from 1 Corinthians 3:11-15,

"For no one can lay a foundation other than that which is laid, which is Jesus Christ. Now if anyone builds on the foundation with gold, silver, precious stones, wood, hay, straw—each one's work will become manifest, for the Day will disclose it, because it will be revealed by fire, and the fire will test what sort of work each one has done. If the work that anyone has built on the foundation survives, he will receive a reward. If anyone's work is burned up, he will suffer loss, though he himself will be saved, but only as through fire."

Paul explains in this passage that for a Christian—especially ministers—his foundation is solid. But what do we use to build upon that solid foundation? Do we use silver, gold and precious stones? Or is our material of choice wood, hay and straw? When tested by fire, which will survive?

Ephesians 5:15-16 says, "Look carefully then how you walk, not as unwise but as wise, making the best use of the time, because the days are evil."

This idea of "redeeming the time" is significant. Time is fleeting. It's uncertain. Whatever amount is lost can never be regained.

This Christian pilgrimage is not to be taken lightly and spent frivolously. What about our lives? Our Christian pilgrimage? Do we follow Christ? Do we strive toward holiness?

Or do we, even as Christians, fall into laziness and complacency? Do we engage in worthless activities of no heavenly value? Or are we busy about the work of Christ?

Edwards here reminds us that someday we shall be shown our works. By urging us to focus on Christ as we journey on, he attempts to keep us from being ashamed on that day. Will our brief span be of eternal value? Or of no value?

4. Consider that those who are willing thus to spend their lives as a journey towards heaven may have heaven.—Heaven, however high and glorious, is

attainable to such poor worthless creatures as we are. We may attain that glorious region which is the habitation of angels: yea, the dwelling-place of the Son of God, and where is the glorious presence of the great Jehovah. And we may have it freely, without money and without price. If we are but willing to travel the road that leads to it and bend our course that way as long as we live, we may and shall have heaven for our eternal resting place.

Don't let that last line fool you. Edwards did not believe in a works theology. He is not saying that if we have enough works along our journey we may go to heaven. He believed in salvation by grace alone, through faith alone, in Christ alone.

So what is he saying? Works do not earn us salvation. But if we are truly saved, our lives will be characterized by works. Good works are a manifestation of salvation— they are not the basis for it.

Again, he describes the glory of heaven made so by the presence of God. Again, he urges us to desire that glorious home as our final destination. He then reminds us that the gift of salvation is free to us, though it was supremely costly to our Savior. Then he encourages us to be busy about following Christ as we complete our journey toward that heavenly home.

5. Let it be considered that if our lives be not a journey towards heaven, they will be a journey to hell. All mankind, after they have been here a short while, go to either of the two great receptacles of all that depart out of this world: the one in *heaven;* whither the bulk of mankind throng. And one or

the other of these must be the issue of our course
in this world.

Our lives can be likened to a room with a doorway at
each end. One doorway leads to heaven; the other leads
to hell. Believers, regardless how hard their struggles,
are drawn by God to the door that leads to heaven. They
were brought to a place of faith in Christ and trusted
in Him as their Savior for the remainder of their lives.

Unbelievers lived their lives following their love
of self. They never turned to the Lord as their Savior.
Perhaps they never even acknowledged His existence!
They may have been good people during their lives—or
perhaps they were monsters plaguing society for the
entirety of their lives. Their end is the same. Either way,
they reach for the only door they can see—the one that
leads to hell.

Each doorway represents death. Every one of us will
pass through one of them. Just a small step and then
eternity. Which door will you open?

*****

Questions for Reflection

1. Would it be a struggle for you to *gladly* exchange anything you have in this life for the glories of heaven? Explain why or why not? What do you think needs to happen for you to be able to do that?
2. For what better purpose can you spend your life than reflecting Christ in every part of it?
3. Do you represent Christ in every aspect of your life? What steps need to be taken to improve that representation?
4. Describe how it feels to come home after a hard day at work, or after a long vacation. Now imagine the joy and relief of coming to the home you were intended to inhabit from before the foundation of the world. Briefly try to describe that feeling.
5. What parts of your life would you label as "wood, hay and straw" and what steps will you take in respect to that realization?

CHAPTER FIVE

CONCLUSION

I shall conclude by giving a few *directions:*

1. Labor to get a sense of the vanity of this world, on account of the little satisfaction that is to be enjoyed here, its short continuance, and unserviceableness when we most stand in need of help, *viz.* on a death-bed.—All men, that live any considerable time in the world, might see enough to convince them of its vanity, if they would but consider.—Be persuaded therefore to exercise consideration when you see and hear, from time to time, of the death of others. Labor to turn your thoughts this way. See the vanity of the world in such a glass.

Some people seem bigger than life, don't they? They are so . . . alive and powerful and have so much to offer the world. Those people have always existed. I imagine King David like this. King Solomon. Paul, the apostle. So many others.

We view some public figures that way in this age. I remember my shock upon hearing about the deaths of John F. Kennedy, Martin Luther King, John F. Kennedy, Jr., and Princess Diana. These people seemed larger than life, somehow.

Some people in my own sphere seem bigger than life. So robust and vibrant. But guess what? They will all die someday, as hard as it is to imagine.

Think about your own life—of the attributes you possess, the gifts God has given you, the vitality of your thinking and movement and approach to living. Someday your heart will beat no more. The essence that makes you who you are will leave the body you've cared for so well. And you will have died. It's astonishing to consider the state of being no more upon this earth.

Then again, consider the greatest life that has ever existed—Jesus Christ, the Son of Almighty God. Talk about bigger than life! Talk about vitality and gifts and love and the most exquisite attributes imaginable. Talk about how much He had to offer the world. And yet, His life ended after a mere thirty-three years. His heart beat no more. His essence (spirit) left that body of flesh. It's no wonder that His disciples were filled with such disbelief and despair afterwards.

Perhaps we have such trouble truly recognizing these things because we can only see this side of heaven— from below. Our knowledge and vision are limited. We comprehend intellectually that the spirit is eternal, yet it's hard to imagine the existence of a world we cannot experience as yet.

Our end will come. Others will be left to ponder an existence without us.

This has been described as a baby still in the womb. All he knows is what surrounds him—darkness, warmth, comfort, silence and liquid. He's got it pretty good there. Yet, he's heard there's another world through a short corridor of birth. In that world is light and cold and noise—but a lot of wonderful things, as well. Would he be willing to trade the known for the unknown?

We're that little baby. We're comfortable where we are. Our lives may not be perfect, but the world around us is a known commodity. We're told about the glories of heaven, yet we tend to cling to the known instead.

Like that little baby, there comes a time when we have no choice but to step through the corridor—and also like that baby we will find a place superior to anything we've known before, a place where we feel more at home than ever, feel more love and joy than ever, and are brought face-to-face with the One who loved us before the creation of the world and breathed life into us—both physically and spiritually. What an astonishing thought.

Do we truly believe? If we don't, we need to get to know our Savior more deeply. If we do, then it won't be a struggle to exchange all we have in this life for that spectacular one to come.

That's what Jonathan Edwards wrote about in this sermon.

2. Labor to be much acquainted with heaven.—If you are not acquainted with it, you will not be likely to spend your life as a journey thither. You will not be sensible of its worth, nor will you long for it. Unless you are much conversant in your mind with a better good, it will be exceeding difficult to you to have your hearts loose from these things, to use them only in subordination to something else, and be ready to part with them for the sake of that better good.—Labor therefore to obtain a realizing

> sense of a heavenly world, to get a firm belief of
> its reality, and to be very much conversant with it
> in your thoughts.

What we know about heaven comes in tiny snippets throughout the Bible. Therefore, if we want to know more about it, we should read our Bibles closely.

John MacArthur wrote a helpful book, *The Glory of Heaven*. He takes those tiny snippets of information and puts them all together like a jigsaw puzzle. Many of the pieces are missing because of the limited information the Bible reveals. Yet, we can benefit from his efforts to piece them all together.

Several other sound theologians have written on the subject. Therefore, don't deny yourself the help they can provide in your understanding of heaven.

As Edwards states, "Labor therefore to obtain a realizing sense of a heavenly world, to get a firm belief of its reality, and to be very much conversant with it in your thoughts."

I might add that the more intimate your relationship with Christ is, the better you'll be able to comprehend what makes heaven the glorious place it is—the presence and dwelling place of our blessed Lord, Jesus Christ. Never stop learning of Him. Never stop pressing forward in your walk with Him.

> 3. Seek heaven only by Jesus Christ.—Christ tells us
>   that he is the way, and the truth, and the life. (John
>   14:65) He tells us that he is the door of the sheep.
>   "I am the door, by me if any man enter in he shall
>   be saved; and go in and out and find pasture."
>   (John 10:9) If we therefore would improve our
>   lives as a journey towards heaven, we must seek

it by him and not by our own righteousness, as expecting to obtain it only for his sake: looking to him having our dependence on him, who has procured it for us by his merit. And expect strength to walk in holiness, the way that leads to heaven, only from him.

4. Let Christians help one another in going this journey.—There are many ways whereby Christians might greatly forward one another in their way to heaven, as by religious conference, etc. Therefore let them be exhorted to go this journey as it were in company: conversing together, and assisting one another. Company is very desirable in a journey, but in none so much as this.—Let them go united and not fall out by the way, which would be to hinder one another, but use all means they can to help each other up the hill.—This would ensure a more successful traveling and a more joyful meeting at their Father's house in glory."

This final aspect of our pilgrimage toward heaven is no less vital than the rest. Fellowship with other brothers and sisters in Christ is important.

Believers are to encourage each other toward this heavenly goal. We are to meditate upon it and share our thoughts with others. It should be a comfortable topic in our conversation. And when someone appears to be approaching that destination before we do, let us come alongside them in love to walk with them along the way.

I've written much about this. I've taught classes on it. I've instructed countless families who were walking this road with their loved ones. So this is a subject near to my heart.

Are we comfortable with death? We'll be comfortable dialoguing with others about it. Do we believe in the glories of heaven? Then encourage each other in the Lord, especially as that time of departure draws near.

A word of caution here. People nearing the end of life sometimes need to talk about it. As the time approaches, they find themselves thinking about it more and more. Sometimes they attempt to talk about it with others. Yet many times, well-meaning family and friends often shut them down when they raise the subject.

"No, no, we're not going to talk like that. We're going to be positive. You're going to get better. Just you wait and see."

They've just missed an opportunity to share closely in their loved one's life and death. Let people talk about these things. Many times, they know they're dying and need someone to share that with. They need to be encouraged to speak, not shut down. This is one of the most important moments of their lives. Share the journey with them. Encourage them in the Lord. Don't miss this sweet opportunity to walk with them at the end.

*****

I wrote this book to showcase what I consider to be one of Jonathan Edwards' best sermons. I've found it intensely encouraging and wanted to encourage others with its timeless message.

To do that, I broke it up into manageable segments about which I could add a few words. However, I also want to give you the gift of seeing his sermon all in one piece—without my interruptions. The next chapter will have it printed in its entirety. Enjoy it and encourage others with it.

CHAPTER SIX

THE CHRISTIAN PILGRIM

OR

THE TRUE CHRISTIAN'S LIFE A JOURNEY TOWARD HEAVEN

by

Jonathan Edwards

Dated September, 1733, 1753.

Preached at Boston and at New Haven; preached to Stockbridge Indians

Hebrews 11:13-14

And confessed that they were strangers and pilgrims on the earth. For they that say such things, declare plainly that they seek a country.

Subject: This life might so to be spent by us as to be only a journey towards heaven.

The apostle is here setting forth the excellencies of the grace of faith, by the glorious effects and happy issue of it in the saints of the Old Testament. He had spoken in the preceding part of the chapter particularly, of Abel, Enoch, Noah, Abraham, and Sarah, Isaac, and Jacob. Having enumerated those instances, he takes notice that "these all died in faith, not having received the promises, but having seen them afar off, were persuaded of them, and embraced them, and confessed that they were strangers," etc.—In these words the apostle seems to have a more particular respect to Abraham and Sarah, and their kindred, who came with them from Haran, and from Ur of the Chaldees, as appears by the 15th verse, where the apostle says, "and truly if they had been mindful of that country from whence they came out, they might have had opportunity to have returned."

Two things may be observed here:

1. What these saints confessed of themselves, *viz. that they were strangers and pilgrims on the earth.*—Thus we have a particular account concerning Abraham, "I am a stranger and a sojourner with you." (Gen. 23:4) And it seems to have been the general sense of the patriarchs, by what Jacob says to Pharaoh. "And Jacob said to Pharaoh, The days of the years of my pilgrimage are an hundred and thirty years; few and evil have the days of years of my life been, and have not attained to the days of the years of the life of my fathers in the days of their pilgrimage." (Gen. 47:9) "I am a stranger and a sojourner with thee as all my fathers were." (Psa. 39:12)

2. The inference that the apostle draws from hence, *viz. that they sought another country as their home.* "For they that say such things, declare plainly that they seek a country." In confessing

that they were strangers, they plainly declared that this is not their country, that this is not the place where they are at home. And in confessing themselves to be pilgrims, they declared plainly that this is not their settled abode, but that they have respect to some other country, which they seek, and to which they are traveling.

SECTION 1

That this life ought to be so spent by us, as to be only a journey or pilgrimage towards heaven.

Here I would observe,

1. That we ought not to rest in the world and its enjoyments, but should desire heaven. We should "seek first the kingdom of God." (Mat. 6:33) We ought above all things to desire a heavenly happiness; to be with God and dwell with Jesus Christ. Though surrounded with outward enjoyments, and settled in families with desirable friends and relations; though we have companions whose society is delightful, and children in whom we see many promising qualifications; though we live by good neighbors, and are generally beloved where known; we ought not to take our rest in these things as our portion. We should be so far from resting in them, that we should desire to leave them all, in God's due time. We ought to possess, enjoy and use them, with no other view but readily to quit them, whenever we are called to it, and to change them willingly and cheerfully for heaven.

A traveler is not wont to rest in what he meets with, however comfortable and pleasing, on the road. If he passes through pleasant places, flowery meadows, or shady groves, he does not take up his fine appearances to put off the thought of proceeding. No, but his journey's end is in his mind. If he meets with comfortable accommodations at an inn, he entertains no thoughts of settling there. He considers that these things are not his own, that he is but a stranger, and when he has refreshed himself, or tarried for a night, he is for going forward. And it is pleasant to him to think that so much of the way is gone.

So should we desire heaven more than the comforts and enjoyments of this life. The apostle mentions it as an encouraging, comfortable consideration to Christians, that they draw nearer their happiness. "Now is our salvation nearer than when we believed."—Our hearts ought to be loose to these things, as that of a man on a journey, that we may as cheerfully part with them whenever God calls. "But this I say, brethren, the time is short, it remaineth, that both they that have wives be as though they had none; and they that weep, as though they wept not; and they that rejoice, as though they rejoiced not; and they that buy, as though they possessed not; and they that use this world, as not abusing it; for the fashion of this world passeth away." (1 Cor. 7:29-31) These things are only lent to us for a little while, to serve a present turn, but we should set our *hearts* on heaven, as our inheritance forever.

2. We ought to seek heaven, by traveling in the way that lead thither. This is a way of holiness. We should choose and desire to travel thither in

the way and in no other, and part with all those carnal appetites which, as weights, will tend to hinder us. "Let us lay aside every weight, and the sin which doth so easily beset us, and let us run with patience the race set before us." (Heb 12:1) However pleasant the gratification of any appetite may be, we must lay it aside if it be a hindrance, or a stumbling block, in the way to heaven.

We should travel on in the way of obedience to all God's commands, even the difficult as well as the easy, denying all our sinful inclinations and interests. The way to heaven is ascending. We must be content to travel up hill, though it be hard and tiresome, and contrary to the natural bias of our flesh. We should follow Christ: the path he traveled, was the right way to heaven. We should take up our cross and follow him, in meekness and lowliness of heart, obedience and charity, diligence to do good, and patience under afflictions. The way to heaven in a heavenly life, an imitation of those who are in heaven in their holy enjoyments, loving, adoring, serving, and praising God and the Lamb. Even if we *could* go to heaven with the gratification of our lusts, we should prefer a way of holiness and conformity to the spiritual self-denying rules of the gospel.

3. We should travel on in this way in a laborious manner.—Long journeys are attended with toil and fatigue, especially if through a wilderness. Persons in such a case expect no other than to suffer hardships and weariness.—So we should travel in this way of holiness, improving our time and strength, to surmount the difficulties and obstacles that are in the way. The land we have to travel through, is a wilderness. There are many

mountains, rocks, and rough places that we must go over, and therefore there is a necessity that we should lay out our strength.

4. Our whole lives ought to be spent in traveling this road.—We ought to begin *early.* This should be the *first* concern, when persons become capable of acting. When they first set out in the *world*, they should set out on this journey.—And we ought to travel on with *assiduity.* It ought to be the work of every day. We should often think of our journey's end; and make it our daily work to travel on in the way that leads to it.—He who is on a journey is often thinking of the destined place, and it is his daily care and business to get along and to improve his time to get towards his journey's end. Thus should heaven be continually in our thoughts, and the immediate entrance or passage to it, *viz.* death, should be present with us.—We ought to *persevere* in this way as long as we live.

    "Let us run with patience the race that is set before us." (Heb. 12:1) Though the road be difficult and toilsome, we must hold out with patience, and be content to endure hardships. Though the journey be long, yet we must not stop short, but hold on till we arrive at the place we seek. Nor should we be discouraged with the length and difficulties of the way, as the children of Israel were, and be for turning back again. All our thought and design should be to press forward till we arrive.

5. We ought to be continually growing in holiness, and in that respect coming nearer and nearer to heaven.—We should be endeavoring to come nearer to heaven, in being more heavenly,

becoming more and more like the inhabitants of heaven in respect of holiness and conformity to God, the knowledge of God and Christ, in clear views of the glory of God, the beauty of Christ, and the excellency of divine things, as we come nearer to the beatific vision—We should labor to be continually growing in divine love—that this may be an increasing flame in our hearts, till they ascend wholly in this flame—in obedience and a heavenly conversation, that we may do the will of God on the earth as the angels do in heaven, in comfort and spiritual joy, in sensible communion with God and Jesus Christ. Our path should be as "the shining light, that shines more and more to the perfect day." (Pro 4:18) We ought to be hungering and thirsting after righteousness: after an increase in righteousness. "As new-born babes, desire the sincere milk of the work, that ye may grow thereby." (1 Pet 2:2) The perfection of heaven should be our mark. "This one thing I do, forgetting those things which are behind, and reaching forth unto those things that are before, I press toward the mark, for the prize of the high calling of God in Christ Jesus." (Phil 3:13-14)

6. All other concerns of life ought to be entirely subordinate to this.—When a man is on a journey, all the steps he takes are subordinated to the aim of getting to his journey's end. And if he carries money or provisions with him, it is to supply him in his journey. So we ought wholly to subordinate all our other business, and all our temporal enjoyments, to this affair of traveling to heaven. When anything we have becomes a clog and hindrance to us, we should quit it immediately. The use of our worldly enjoyments

and possessions, should be with such a view, and in such a manner as to further us in our way heavenward. Thus we should eat, and drink, and clothe ourselves, and improve the conversation and enjoyment of friends. And whatever business we are settling about, whatever design we are engaging in, we should inquire with ourselves, whether this business or undertaking will forward us in our way to heaven? And if not, we should quit our design.

SECTION II

Why the Christian's life is a journey, or pilgrimage?

1.   This world is not our abiding place. Our continuance here is but very short. Man's days on the earth, are as a shadow. It was never designed by God that this world should be our home. Neither did God give us these temporal accommodations for that end. If God has given us ample estates, and children, or other pleasant friends, it is with no such design, that we should be furnished here, as for a settled abode, but with a design that we should use them for the present, and then leave them in a very little time. When we are called to any secular business, or charged with the care of a family, if we improve our lives to any other purpose than as a journey toward heaven, all our labor will be lost. If we spend our lives in the pursuit of a temporal happiness, as riches or sensual pleasures, credit and esteem from men, delight in our children and the prospect of seeing them well brought up and well settled, etc.—all

these things will be of little significancy to us. Death will blow up all our hopes, and will put an end to these enjoyments. "The places that have known us, will know us no more" and "the eye that has seen us, shall see us no more." We must be taken away forever from all these things, and it is uncertain when: it may be soon after we are put into the possession of them. And then, where will be all our worldly employments and enjoyments, when we are laid in the silent grave! "So man lieth down, and riseth not again, till the heavens be no more." (Job 14:12)

2. The future world was designed to be our settled and everlasting abode. There it was intended that we should be fixed, and there alone is a lasting habitation and a lasting inheritance. The present state is short and transitory, but our state in the other world is everlasting. And as we are there at first, so we must be without change. Our state in the future world, therefore, being eternal, is of so much greater importance than our state here, that all our concerns in this world should be wholly subordinated to it.

3. Heaven is that place alone where our highest end and highest good is to be obtained. God hath made us for himself. "Of him, and through him, and to him are all things." Therefore, then do we attain to our highest end, when we are brought to God: but that is by being brought to heaven, for that is God's throne, the place of his special presence. There is but a very imperfect union with God to be had in this world, a very imperfect knowledge of him in the midst of much darkness: a very imperfect conformity to God, mingled

with abundance of estrangement. Here we can serve and glorify God, but in a very imperfect manner: our service being mingled with sin, which dishonors God.—But when we get to heaven (if ever that be), we shall be brought to a perfect union with God and have more clear views of him. There we shall be fully conformed to God, without any remaining sin: for "we shall see him as he is." There we shall serve God perfectly and glorify him in an exalted manner, even to the utmost of the powers and capacity of our nature. Then we shall perfectly give up ourselves to God: our hearts will be pure and holy offerings, presented in a flame of divine love.

God is the highest good of the reasonable creature, and the enjoyment of him is the only happiness with which our souls can be satisfied.— To go to heaven fully to enjoy God, is *infinitely* better than the most pleasant accommodations here. Fathers and mothers, husbands, wives, children, or the company of earthly friends, are but shadows. But the enjoyment of God is the substance. These are but scattered beams, but God is the sun. These are but streams, but God is the fountain. These but drops, but God is the ocean.—Therefore it becomes us to spend this life only as a journey towards heaven, as it becomes us to make the seeking of our highest end and proper good, the whole work of our lives, to which we should subordinate all other concerns of life. Why should we labor for, or set our hearts on anything else, but that which is our proper end, and true happiness?

4. Our present state, and all that belongs to it, is designed by him that made all things, to be

wholly in order to another world.—This world was made for a place of preparation for another. Man's mortal life was given him that he might be prepared for his fixed state. And all that God has here given us, is given to this purpose. The sun shines, the rain falls upon us, and the earth yields her increase to us for this end. Civil, ecclesiastical, and family affairs, and all our personal concerns, are designed and ordered in subordination to a future world, by the maker and disposer of all things. To this therefore they ought to be subordinated by us.

SECTION III

Instruction afforded by the consideration, that life is a journey or pilgrimage, towards heaven.

1. This doctrine may teach us moderation in our mourning for the loss of such dear friends, who while they lived, improved their lives to right purposes. If they lived a holy life, then their lives were a journey towards heaven. And why should we be immoderate in mourning, when they are got to their journey's end? Death, though it appears to us with a frightful aspect, is to them a great blessing. Their end is happy, and better than their beginning. "The day of their death, is better than the day of their births." (Ecc 7:1) While they lived, they desired heaven, and chose it above this world or any of its enjoyments. For this they earnestly longed, and why should we grieve that they have obtained it?—Now they have got to their Father's house. They find more comfort a thousand times

now they are gone home, than they did in their journey. In this world they underwent much labor and toil: it was a wilderness they passed through. There were many difficulties in the way: mountains and rough places. It was laborious and fatiguing to travel the road, and they had many wearisome days and nights: but now they have got to their everlasting rest. "And I heard a voice from heaven, saying unto me, Write, blessed are the dead which die in the Lord from henceforth: yea, saith the Spirit, that they may rest from their labors; and their works do follow them." (Rev 14;13) They look back upon the difficulties, and sorrows, and dangers of life, rejoicing that they have surmounted them all.

We are ready to look upon death as their calamity, and to mourn that those who were so dear to us should be in the dark grave: that they are there transformed to corruption and worms, taken away from their dear children and enjoyments, etc. as though they were in awful circumstances. But this is owing to our infirmity. They are in a happy condition, inconceivably blessed. They do not mourn, but rejoice with exceeding joy: their mouths are filled with joyful songs, and they drink at rivers of pleasure. They find no mixture of grief that they have changed their earthly enjoyments, and the company of mortals, for heaven. Their life here, though in the best circumstances, was attended with much that was adverse and afflictive, but now there is an end to all adversity. "They shall hunger no more nor thirst any more; neither shall the sun light on them, nor any heat. For the Lamb which is in the midst of the throne, shall feed them and shall lead them unto living fountains of waters: and God shall wipe away all tears from their eyes." (Rev 7:16-17)

It is true, we shall see them no more in this world, yet we ought to consider that we are traveling towards the same place; and why should we break our hearts that they have got there before us? We are following after them, and hope as soon as we get to our journey's end, to be with them again, in better circumstances. A degree of mourning for near relations when departed is not inconsistent with Christianity, but very agreeable to it. For as long as we are flesh and blood, we have animal propensities and affections. But we have just reason that our mourning should be mingled with joy. "But I would not have you to be ignorant, brethren, concerning them that are asleep, that ye sorrow not, even as others that have no hope:" (1 Thes 4:13) *i.e.* that they should not sorrow as the heathen, who had no knowledge of a future happiness. This appears by the following verse; "for if we believe that Jesus died and rose again, even so them also which sleep in Jesus, will God bring with him."

2.   If our lives ought to be only a journey towards heaven, how ill do they improve their lives, that spend them in traveling towards hell?—Some men spend their whole lives, from their infancy to their dying day, in going down the broad way to destruction. They not only draw nearer to hell as to time, but they every day grow more ripe for destruction. They are more assimilated to the inhabitants of the internal world. While others press forward in the straight and narrow way to life and laboriously travel up the hill toward Zion, against the inclinations and tendency of the flesh,

these run with a swift career down to eternal death. This is the employment of every day, with all wicked men, and the whole day is spent in it. As soon as ever they awake in the morning, they set out anew in the way to hell and spend every waking moment in it. They begin in early days. "The wicked are estranged from the womb, they go astray as soon as they are born, speaking lies." (Psa 58:3) They hold on it with perseverance. Many of them who live to be old, are never weary in it. Though they live to be an hundred years old, they will not cease traveling in the way to hell till they arrive there. And all the concerns of life are subordinated to this employment. A wicked man is a servant of sin, his powers and faculties are employed in the service of sin and in fitness for hell. And all his possessions are so used by him as to be subservient to the same purpose. Men spend their time in treasuring up wrath against the day of wrath. Thus do all unclean persons, who live in lascivious practices in secret: all malicious persons, all profane persons that neglect the duties of religion. Thus do all unjust persons, and those who are fraudulent and oppressive in their dealings. Thus do all backbiters and revilers, all covetous persons that set their hearts chiefly on the riches of this world. Thus do tavern-haunters, and frequenters of evil company, and many other kinds that might be mentioned. Thus the bulk of mankind are hastening onward in the broad way to destruction, which is, as it were, filled up with the multitude that are going in it with one accord. And they are every day going to hell out of this broad way by thousands. Multitudes are continually flowing down into the great lake of fire and brimstone, as some mighty river constantly disembogues its water into the ocean.

3. Hence when persons are converted they do but begin their work and set out in the way they have to go.—They never till then do anything at that work in which their whole lives ought to be spent. Persons before conversion never take a step that way. Then does a man first set out on his journey, when he is brought home to Christ, and so far is he from having done his work, that his care and labor in his Christian work and business, is then but begun, in which he must spend the remaining part of his life.

Those persons do ill, who when they are converted and have obtained a hope of their being in a good condition, do not strive as earnestly as they did before, while they were under awakenings. They ought, henceforward, as long as they live, to be as earnest and laborious, as watchful and careful as ever: yea, they should increase more and more. It is no just excuse that now they have obtained conversion. Should not we be as diligent as that we ourselves may be that we may serve and glorify God, happy? And if we have obtained grace, yet we ought to strive as much that we may obtain the other degrees that are before, as we did to obtain that small degree that is behind. The apostle tells us that he forgot what was behind and reached forth towards what was before. (Phil 3:13)

Yea, those who are converted have now a further reason to strive for grace. For they have seen something of its excellency. A man who has once tasted the blessings of Canaan, has more reason to press towards it than he had before. And they who are converted, should strive to "make their calling and election sure." All those who are converted are not sure of it, and those who are sure, do not know that they shall be always so, and still, seeking and serving God with the utmost diligence, is the way to have assurance and to have it maintained.

SECTION IV

An exhortation so to spend the present life, that it may only be a journey towards heaven

Labor to obtain such a disposition of mind that you may choose heaven for your inheritance and home, and may earnestly long for it and be willing to change this world, and all its enjoyments, for heaven. Labor to have your heart taken up so much about heaven, and heavenly enjoyments, as that you may rejoice when God calls you to leave your best earthly friends and comforts for heaven, there to enjoy God and Christ.

Be persuaded to travel in the way that leads to heaven: *viz.* in holiness, self-denial, mortification, obedience to all the commands of God, following Christ's example in a way of a heavenly life, or imitation of the saints and angels in heaven. Let it be your daily work, from morning till night, and all other concerns be subordinated to this. Consider the reasons that have been mentioned why you should thus spend your life: that this world is not your abiding place, that the future world is to be your everlasting abode, and that the enjoyments and concerns of this world are given entirely in order to another. And consider further for motive.

1. How worthy is heaven that your life should be wholly spent as a journey towards it.—To what better purpose can you spend your life, whether you respect your duty or your interest? What better end can you propose to your journey, than to obtain heaven? You are placed in this world with a choice given you, that you may travel which way you please, and one way leads to heaven. Now, can you direct your course better than this way? All men have some aim or other in living. Some mainly seek worldly things. They spend their days in such pursuits. But is not heaven, where is fullness of joy forever, much more worthy to be sought by you? How can you better employ your strength, use your means, and spend your days, than in traveling the road that leads to the everlasting enjoyment of God: to his glorious presence. to the new Jerusalem, to the heavenly mount Zion, where all your desires will be filled and no danger of ever losing your happiness?—No man is at home in this world, whether he choose heaven or not: here he is but a transient person. Where can you choose your home better than in heaven?

2. This is the way to have death comfortable to us.— To spend our lives so as to be only a journeying towards heaven, is the way to be free from bondage and to have the prospect and forethought of death comfortable. Does the traveler think of his journey's end with fear and terror? Is terrible to him to think that he has almost got to his journeys end? Were the children of Israel sorry after forty years' travel in the wilderness, when they had almost got to Canaan? This is the way to be able to part with the world without grief. Does

it grieve the traveler when he has got home, to quit his staff and load of provisions that he had to sustain him by the way?

3. No more of your life will be pleasant to think of when you come to die, than has been spent after this manner.—If you have spent none of your life this way, your whole life will be terrible to you to think of, unless you die under some great delusion. You will see then, that all of your life that has been spent otherwise, is lost. You will then see the vanity of all other aims that you may have proposed to yourself. The thought of what you here possessed and enjoyed will not be pleasant to you, unless you can think also that you have subordinated them to this purpose.

4. Consider that those who are willing thus to spend their lives as a journey towards heaven may have heaven.—Heaven, however high and glorious, is attainable to such poor worthless creatures as we are. We may attain that glorious region which is the habitation of angels: yea, the dwelling-place of the Son of God, and where is the glorious presence of the great Jehovah. And we may have it freely, without money and without price. If we are but willing to travel the road that leads to it and bend our course that way as long as we live, we may and shall have heaven for our eternal resting place.

5. Let it be considered that if our lives be not a journey towards heaven, they will be a journey to hell. All mankind, after they have been here a short while, go to either of the two great receptacles of all that depart out of this world: the one in *heaven*, whither the bulk of mankind throng. And one or

the other of these must be the issue of our course in this world.

I shall conclude by giving a few *directions:*

1. Labor to get a sense of the vanity of this world, on account of the little satisfaction that is to be enjoyed here, its short continuance, and unserviceableness when we most stand in need of help, *viz.* on a death-bed.—All men, that live any considerable time in the world, might see enough to convince them of its vanity, if they would but consider.—Be persuaded therefore to exercise consideration when you see and hear, from time to time, of the death of others. Labor to turn your thoughts this way. See the vanity of the world in such a glass.

2. Labor to be much acquainted with heaven.—If you are not acquainted with it, you will not be likely to spend your life as a journey thither. You will not be sensible of its worth, nor will you long for it. Unless you are much conversant in your mind with a better good, it will be exceeding difficult to you to have your hearts loose from these things, to use them only in subordination to something else, and be ready to part with them for the sake of that better good.—Labor therefore to obtain a realizing sense of a heavenly world, to get a firm belief of its reality, and to be very much conversant with it in your thoughts.

3. Seek heaven only by Jesus Christ.—Christ tells us that he is the way, and the truth, and the life. (John 14:6) He tells us that he is the door of the sheep. "I am the door, by me if any man enter in he shall be saved; and go in and out and find pasture."

(John 10:9) If we therefore would improve our lives as a journey towards heaven, we must seek it by him and not by our own righteousness, as expecting to obtain it only for his sake: looking to him having our dependence on him, who has procured it for us by his merit. And expect strength to walk in holiness, the way that leads to heaven, only from him.

4. Let Christians help one another in going this journey.—There are many ways whereby Christians might greatly forward one another in their way to heaven, as by religious conference, etc. Therefore let them be exhorted to go this journey as it were in company: conversing together, and assisting one another. Company is very desirable in a journey, but in none so much as this.—Let them go united and not fall out by the way, which would be to hinder one another, but use all means they can to help each other up the hill.—This would ensure a more successful traveling and a more joyful meeting at their Father's house in glory.

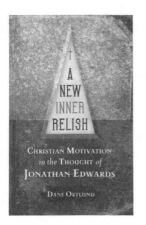

A New Inner Relish

Christian Motivation in the Thought of Jonathan Edwards

Dane Ortlund

What made Jonathan Edwards tick? Dane Ortlund shows us that Edwards was gripped, spellbound by what he saw in God – and that underscored everything he did. Such motivation is essential to authentic Christian living.

"Dane does a marvelous job of demonstrating how the "new sense of the heart," divinely and graciously imparted by God, governs Edwards' understanding of motivation in Christian obedience. I highly recommend Ortlund's clear and insightful study of it"

Sam Storms
Lead Pastor, Bridgeway Church,
Oklahoma City, Oklahoma

ISBN: 978-1-84550-349-9

Christian Focus Publications

Our mission statement –

STAYING FAITHFUL

In dependence upon God we seek to impact the world through literature faithful to His infallible Word, the Bible. Our aim is to ensure that the Lord Jesus Christ is presented as the only hope to obtain forgiveness of sin, live a useful life and look forward to heaven with Him.

Our books are published in four imprints:

CHRISTIAN FOCUS

Popular works including biographies, commentaries, basic doctrine and Christian living.

CHRISTIAN HERITAGE

Books representing some of the best material from the rich heritage of the church.

MENTOR

Books written at a level suitable for Bible College and seminary students, pastors, and other serious readers. The imprint includes commentaries, doctrinal studies, examination of current issues and church history.

CF4•K

Children's books for quality Bible teaching and for all age groups: Sunday school curriculum, puzzle and activity books; personal and family devotional titles, biographies and inspirational stories – because you are never too young to know Jesus!

Christian Focus Publications Ltd,
Geanies House, Fearn, Ross-shire,
IV20 1TW, Scotland, United Kingdom.
www.christianfocus.com